LOXLEY

Wanderings in a Curious Valley

by Peter Machan

Clink Street

For Lilly, Caitlyn and Rose
who live there.

All photographs, drawings and illustrations are by
the author unless otherwise attributed.

Thanks to Steve Draper, John Austin, Jill Jesson, Angie Shaw and Malcolm
Nunn for helping in the making of this book.

Contents

The Birth of Curiosity

Curiouser and curiouser, cried Alice

I have a tendency to collect things. I suppose it's in my nature; part of my very being. It's not something I choose to do but it's something I have to choose very hard not to do. Once I have more than one of any item I find myself almost unconsciously looking around for others to add to it; and that's the start of a collection. I'm not very systematic about it and I'm not really interested in completeness. My interests are thankfully far too eclectic for my condition to become an obsession (though others may disagree). Collections have insinuated themselves into every room in the house, not fine artworks, antique clocks or Chinese porcelain but bleached white bird skulls picked up on Norfolk beaches, various interesting feathers and shells of all shapes, sizes and colours from all over the world, occupying glass shelves around the walls of the bathroom; coins, stamps, fossils, cigarette cards and handmade pocket knives in drawers in the study. Stuffed owls look down from the top of the wardrobe, in which hang theatrical costumes, and books line just about every wall throughout the house. Collections extend into the garden where over a hundred pots house a prized collection of hostas and the greenhouse is full of cacti. My granddaughter, Lilly, calls all this, with the frank insensitivity of a six-year-old, Grandad's 'stuff'.

This trait was manifested early. At my primary school, as was the case with all young lads in the 50s, collecting was central to our relationships. Your standing in the schoolyard, which was far too steep for football, depended on the skill with which deals and swops could be negotiated. It was a dog-eat-dog little world in which the strongest could boast of their completed 'Bird Portraits' album of PG Tips Tea cards having intimidated a younger child into exchanging a prized, and virtually unobtainable, 'peregrine falcon' for a couple of the most common cards and pretending that he was doing him an enormous favour. Marbles, I remember, were another popular medium of exchange and conkers in season, and of course every boy collected stamps.

By the time I was nine or ten like most kids at this time, I enjoyed a freedom that would be quite alien to the way of life of children today. Without such distractions as daytime TV, electronic devices and the fear of heavy traffic or 'Stranger Danger' we would be let loose at weekends and holidays to roam. We spent whole days exploring the woodlands and bombed out sites within walking distance and, having no interest in sport or football, would often spend all day just wandering the streets of Sheffield, discovering new places and collecting bits and pieces. I have no idea where my mother thought we were but I do know that we never told her. In summer we would take a 'picnic' a few bits of fruit and a biscuit and fishing nets to trawl for sticklebacks in a pond in the woods or torment the frogs that lived in the stream. In spring we would bring back jars full of frog and toad spawn and watch it swarm into tadpoles in the washing-up bowl ponds that we loved to build, dreaming of one day building a zoo.

It was at this stage that I built my first 'cabinet'. We were fortunate in having a sort of carriage house and outbuildings at the top of the garden. Our grandfather, who lived with us, occupied the tool shed and greenhouse, and the large garage housed our green Morris Minor, but we three boys were given free run of the rest. The garage had a sort of hayloft above, reached through a narrow, square trap door from a wooden ladder set into the wall, making it completely inaccessible to adults. Many happy hours were spent up there in our 'den' but the best part was a tiny room at the far end above the tool shed to which access could be gained only by crawling through a low triangular doorway below the sloping eves. At the bottom of the half round window in the gable wall of this little space was a row of half-round openings, the clue to the fact that the former occupants were pigeons. Here I built my first 'Cabinet of Curiosities' although at the time I wouldn't have recognised the term and I called it, somewhat grandiosely, 'The Natural History Museum'. Anyone braving the tortuous squeeze into the space would have been underwhelmed by the exhibits; a few bird's eggs, pinecones and feathers, shells gathered on trips to Cleethorpes, some pebbles and an interestingly contorted bedspring together with various items purloined from the rest of the house; an old banjo and a zebra skin rug. From a jumble sale at the local church I acquired my most curious exhibit, an elephant's tooth! I don't recall having any paying visitors!

A favourite destination of my more urban wanderings was Sheffield City Museum in Weston Park where my passion for curiosities of all kinds had free reign. During the 1950s and 60s the museum displays were of the traditional order; a gallery full of row upon row of dark wood and glass cabinets of stuffed animals and birds, a long wall on which hung an eclectic collection of South Sea Island miscellanea, and tall glass cases displaying human skulls, pottery and weapons recovered during nineteenth century excavations of Derbyshire barrows. All of these I found fascinating but the greatest treasures of all were those hidden away in the racks of wide wooden drawers that could be slid open to reveal collections of multicoloured butterflies pinned in neat rows, iridescent beetles or, the best of all, hundreds of shells, of all sizes and shapes, from all over the world. I would spend illicit hours opening the drawers one after the other in the certain knowledge that this wasn't really allowed and expecting that a uniformed attendant would be tapping me on the shoulder at any moment. It still gives me a frisson remembering such delightful childhood expeditions.

I still wander and even now rarely venture forth without discovering something new and interesting. The displays of 'Museums Sheffield' have, of course, long since been 'modernised' and I doubt that visitors still experience the same sense of wonder that sparked my lifetime fascination with nature as did the 'Cabinet of Curiosities' that was the old Weston Park, although there are still drawers of beetles and butterflies to discover.

Sheffield does, however, still display a couple of particularly curious collections. John Ruskin, the nineteenth-century art critic, had an admiration for the craftsmanship of the town's cutlers and silversmiths, and created a body named 'The Guild of St George' to which he donated a collection of his material. This was housed in buildings firstly at Walkley and later in Meersbrook Park where, I was told, there had been peacocks. This curious collection, under the auspices of the Guild of St George, is now displayed in its own gallery next to the new Winter Gardens in the city centre. Visitors to the Ruskin Collection are either enchanted or bemused by the wonderfully eclectic mix of exhibits, including early Renaissance art, gothic architecture, plaster casts of decorative details from buildings, mineral and geological samples, engravings, mosaic decoration, illustrations of birds, flowers, insects, geological specimens, illustrated books and medieval manuscripts. Just my sort of collection.

A clue to the second, and most curious of all Sheffield's present day collections, can be spotted by anyone casting their eyes upwards, to where, high on the red brick wall of one of the buildings of Sheffield University, there is a most remarkable and unexpected stone relief; the depiction of an anteater rummaging around in a termite's nest!

The building in question was built to house the Department of Biology, the professor of which, at the end of the 19th century when it was built, was the remarkable Alfred Denny who created such a massive collection of anatomical specimens that it originally occupied three galleried floors of the University's Firth Hall atrium. This fabulous collection was for many years stored away until, in 2012, a new home was found for it in a large room on the second floor of the building that is now named after Alfred Denny. The experience on entering this display space is breath taking; sheer sensory overload. Skeletons of every conceivable animal, bird and reptile are sensitively poised in free standing glass cases so that they can be viewed from all sides; monkeys and marmosets, seals and squid, ostrich, pelicans and kangaroos. It was only recently that I discovered the museum, it only opens for booked tours on the first Saturday in the month, but I've a feeling that if this inspirational collection had been available to view when I was a child it may well have changed my life.

The finest local example of a true Cabinet of Curiosities was to be found tucked away in a tiny traditionally-built lead miners' cottage in the nearby village of Castleton in the Peak District. A wooden signboard affixed to the wall outside grandiosely proclaimed this to be the home of 'The Douglas House of Wonders'. One Saturday, having ridden out to Castleton on our bikes, my brother and I decided to investigate. As I remember it you entered by the low cottage doorway beside which a sort of dark ticket booth had been erected and an aged lady, who turned out to be Mrs Douglas, could be vaguely discerned in the gloom, peered out through bottle-bottom thick glasses to accept the small entrance fee. We were then asked to wait behind the blackout curtaining that shrouded the doorway to the interior exhibition rooms before she emerged with a torch and proceeded to personally conduct a guided tour of the extraordinary collection of exhibits. Mr Douglas, who had since died, it transpired, had been a noted model maker, electrical engineer and magician. We couldn't contain our glee as the flickering torchlight was shone on an 'Isometric Scale Model of the Shredded Wheat Factory at Welwyn Garden City', a miniature greenhouse complete with plants ("Can you spot the greenfly?"), The Lord's Prayer that fitted through the eye of a needle and the smallest electric motor in the world. Up the stairs in the tiny bedroom on a wooden table was a broken model of the Taj Mahal, a miner's boot, a collection of 'native weapons' and locks and keys, none of which matched. Each had its own curled brown cardboard label affixed by string on which the name was written in spidery black ink. It was a complete delight and it was a sad day indeed when the old lady died and the unique attraction closed. Most of the exhibits do survive, however, and can be seen in Castleton Visitor Centre and Buxton Museum. But it's not the same.

The remarkable House of Wonders in Castleton was part of a long tradition of cabinets of curiosity stretching back to sixteenth-century Italy where such noblemen as Ferrante Imperato of Naples would delight in displaying their learning by making elaborate collections of natural history subjects and books in a specially adapted room where every surface, including the vaulted ceiling, from which a stuffed crocodile was suspended, was occupied with preserved fishes, stuffed mammals and curious shells. Corals were displayed on the bookcases in which stacks of books preserved his herbarium. The idea of a 'cabinet' being a piece of furniture only came later.

Curious Places

From the middle ages the earliest travel writers approached their subject in just this fashion. One of the very first books describing Britain's landscape was *Polychronicon* (meaning 'many stories') compiled in 1387 by Ranulf Higden, a Benedictine monk. It is a mixture of fact and fiction, myth and legend, knowledge and invented explanations for the inexplicable; a veritable cabinet of curiosities. He was particularly fascinated by certain peculiar features of our neighbouring area of the Peak District of Derbyshire:

> In Britain there are many wonders. Nevertheless, four are the most
> wonderful. The first is the Peak. There such a strong wind blows
> out of the cracks in the earth, that it throws against cloths that men
> threw up.

I'm with him there in regarding certain features of the Peak District as being most curious, and so are the many writers who were to follow him throughout the centuries. William Camden, writing in his *Britannia* in 1586, whilst being dismissive of some of the more far-fetched traveller's tales of the Peak country, illustrates what he calls his *'remarkables of this hilly rough country'* in verse:

Nine Things that please us in the Peak we see,
A cave, a Den, a Hole, the Wonder be;
Lead, Sheep and Pasture are the useful Three.
Chatsworth and Castle, and the Bath delight;
Much more you see, all little worth the sight.

Thomas Hobbes, who became tutor to William Cavendish at Chatsworth in 1608, pared the list of Camden's nine 'wonders' down to his famous seven namely; Eldon Hole, the wells at Buxton, Mam Tor, the Ebbing and Flowing well at Tideswell, Poole's Cavern, Peak Cavern and Chatsworth House.

Daniel Defoe, during his journey into the Peak in about 1720, was keen to experience them fully and made detours around the county in order to do so. Being a man of the Enlightenment, however, with a particular interest in reporting on the economy and industry of the places he visited on his three tours of England and Scotland, he was thoroughly dismissive of most of the 'so called wonders' as being simply natural phenomena that could be replicated elsewhere. Only the Eldon Hole, that was at the time considered bottomless, and Chatsworth House, that stood *"on the edge of a howling wilderness,"* would he accept as worthy of being called wonders. Instead he drew attention to what he would consider worthy of special note. He was especially astonished, for example, to witness a lead miner appear from the depths of a shaft in a field near Wirksworth and to be entertained by his family that lived happily in *"a large hollow cave, which the poor people, by two curtains hanged across, had parted into two rooms."* Today, fortunately, lead miners and their families can no longer be discovered living in caves, or anywhere else in the Peak and such features as those selected by Hobbes as 'wonders' can now be rationally explained, but it doesn't detract from the Peak District's unique appeal, and such considerations haven't dampened the enthusiasm of the many thousands of visitors to the Peak District who are attracted to the curiosities of the landscape, its traditions and its history.

The Curious Valley

The broad valley of the River Loxley, which lies to the north-west of Sheffield, much of it within the Peak District National Park, may not exhibit the sort of features that could be called 'wonders' but it has enough curiosities to fill any cabinet; features of its geology and history, curious events, tales, customs and traditions, and an unparalleled range of habitats and environments, natural and manmade. As in any assemblage of curiosities, this collection of apparently random, unrelated features in the space of one valley renders them interesting in themselves and the whole collection fascinating. The whole valley was formerly part of the huge Parish of Bradfield, the largest in area in England, and, following Sheffield City boundary extensions in 1901, 1967 and 1974, is now entirely within the Sheffield City boundary. Despite this it's a place that has always had its own quite distinct identity, been somewhat cut off, and still seems out of sync with the modern world, making the Loxley Valley an intriguing place. During this strange year of 2020 I have been able to explore places within it that I'd never discovered before. Every time I've been able to get out for a walk there I've discovered something new, a natural feature or something manmade, an event or a story. My fascination for assembling and organising curiosities of all kinds has spurred my interest in the Loxley Valley and underpins this book.

I've never lived in the valley but I went to school there, as a sixth form pupil in the mid nineteen sixties, when I was transferred from the small grammar school on the opposite side of the city to what was then called Myers Grove, a new comprehensive of nearly 2,000 pupils seeking to establish itself amidst Sheffield's radical reorganisation of secondary education. Although the experience was a shock to the system I came into contact with some inspirational teachers, including Mel Jones, the Geography teacher who shared my interests in discovering local stories and remained a friend throughout his life. Years later I was to spend a number of years as the head teacher in one of the local primary schools. Now my daughter and her family live deep within the valley and I've had the time to get to know it better and marvel at its strangeness.

1

Introducing the Curious Valley

It rises near the village of Bradfield and flows along a thinly-peopled country, which in the memory of man was wholly unenclosed and uncultivated, called Loxley-Chase; a district which seems to have the fairest pretensions to be the Locksley of our old ballads, where was born that redoubtable hero Robin Hood.

JOSEPH HUNTER, 1819

The River Loxley and its Valley

The River Loxley is one of the turbulent streams that tumble through wide valleys from their headwaters in the high Pennine moorlands in the west to meet the River Don as it flows southwards towards Sheffield city centre before turning towards the east. Daniel Defoe, during his tour through England in 1724, reached the area at a time, like that in 2019, when the Don was in flood.

> The River Don, with its rapid terrible current, had swelled its banks, and done a prodigious deal of damage… for this river is of kin to the Derwent for the fierceness of its streams, beginning in the same western mountains, pouring down their waters with such fury into these great rivers, their streams are so rapid that nothing is able to stand in their way.

There are four of these tributary streams that meet the Don within the city boundary, the Loxley, the Porter, the Rivelin and the Sheaf, the latter from which the city takes its name. The western edges of Sheffield's suburbs climb the ridges and steep hillsides between the valleys, whilst their valley floors, mostly green and wooded, extend like green corridors of parkland between the suburbs and well into the city itself. These rivers, still beaded with mill ponds, represent the source of the power that generated the industrial wealth of the area, for they were all adapted centuries ago to provide power for dozens of mills, mainly for metal-working. On the foundation of inherited skills and craftsmanship within these valleys' cutlery mills the city's steel industry was forged. Each valley, however, has its own quite distinct character. The valley of the Sheaf forms a southern gateway for road and rail, and, like the valleys of the Porter and the Rivelin, is deeply wooded. A string of very popular urban parks follows the Porter from Hunters Bar whilst the Rivelin Valley is more rugged and less frequented. The most northerly valley of these streams, the Loxley Valley, is the widest, longest and most rural, akin to one of the Yorkshire Dales.

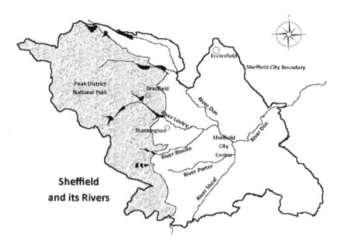

Sheffield
and its Rivers

The upper Loxley Valley, which above Bradfield is known as Bradfield Dale, takes its waters from a huge bowl-like expanse of moorland that reaches to the western watershed along the Derbyshire border at Derwent Edge; ideal water-gathering grounds to fill the four major reservoirs, which, built by the Sheffield Water Company in the mid-nineteenth century, still supply much of the city's needs. Fed by dozens of moorland rivulets, the infant Loxley flows north-east in a wide, open valley before reaching Low Bradfield, where it turns to a south-easterly direction for about six kilometres to meet its confluence with the Rivelin at Malin Bridge, before continuing through Hillsborough to meet the Don. The whole valley is now within the Sheffield City boundary and the boundary of the Peak District National Park extends eastwards to include the broad basin of Bradfield Dale. Whilst most of the lower valley is narrow, wooded and besmirched with industrial remains the upper valley is broad, rural and agricultural in nature. The rectangularly-patterned hillsides are surprisingly green, most of the fields being used as grazing land for sheep in the upper valley and cattle lower down.

No main roads run either through or across it although it is served by a network of local roads and winding narrow lanes. The upper reaches feel remote and are unfamiliar to most people, making this one of my favourite places to roam. Even today, despite being within the boundary of one of the country's largest cities, the valley, hemmed in on all sides by steep slopes and craggy hillsides, has a remoteness and feeling of semi-isolation. The whole valley is somewhat isolated from the rest of the city. *"Went there to visit a friend once, on arrival looked around and thought we'd taken a wrong turning and ended up in Wales"* writes a recent correspondent on a chat forum. A teacher at Dungworth School within the valley, on resigning her post in the early 1900s commented *"One has to reside in a place like Dungworth to understand the misery of enforced idleness!"*

Much of the valley is designated Green Belt. During the 1950s and 60s a local bus company called 'Sheffield United Tours' ran Sunday excursions around the area in their red and white coaches, dubbing it 'Sheffield's Lakeland'. Today most people heading out from Sheffield for a Sunday walk make straight out to the Peak District's Hope Valley and beyond, bypassing these 'Lake District' valleys. In the last couple of years, however, the attractiveness of the area in terms of its wildlife, heritage of farming and forestry and its recreational opportunities has been increasingly recognised. Sheffield and Rotherham Wildlife Trust has been successful in a bid to the National Lottery Heritage Fund for £2.6 million to oversee the work of more than twenty partner organisations as 'The Sheffield Lakeland Landscape Partnership', a sixty-year-old concept that is being rightly revived. The Trust will have plenty to coordinate as there is a rich variety of habitats and ecosystems within the valley; rivers, streams and open water, ancient woodlands and conifer plantations, rocky outcrops and disused mine workings, heather moorlands, raised bogs and wildflower hay meadows.

People of the Valley

The people who live in the valley, of whom many trace their local ancestry for generations, feel a strong local attachment and there is a close sense of community akin to that in such rural sparsely populated locations as the

Yorkshire Dales or the Lake District. There are local families that have never extended far beyond the area. David Hey, the local historian and researcher into family names, has traced the Dungworth family history, for example, back to 1323 when William Dungworth, the son of Anne Dungworth, was recorded as taking possession of a small farm at Storrs, near the village of Dungworth. Members of the Dungworth family still live nearby and the name has never travelled much further afield. Family and community memories here are long. Whenever someone posts a local picture of 'days gone by' on the local Facebook page; a family posing in Sunday best outside a farmhouse, a farmer ploughing with horses, or a steam lorry delivering milk, there invariably follows a string of reminiscences and stories about the family members depicted in the photograph. *"Such a wonderful place; interlocked history and story. We were all a small part of the most wonderful live local history. We were so privileged to be part of the stories from around those villages, farms and brickyards, so many characters so many stories"* is a typical response to such images. *"Most of the older locals were interesting and characterful which is lost today as we don't have the same gatherings of Sunday School, Village Hall, pubs and events that we had back then when most were related to each other"* is the nostalgic response of another.

There is no lack of local 'characters' to be subject to such reminiscences. Typically, Joe Turner of Hilltop above Dungworth, born in 1901, is still remembered despite having died in 1981. He managed at various times and opportunities to combine the local trades of hawker, clay miner, leatherworker, clog maker and whip maker with his regular occupation of selling fruit and vegetables by horse and cart and later by lorry. His principal interest, however, was in horses, in all aspects of which he was expert. When he was eighty the local newspaper ran an illustrated feature on his unique, lifetime's collection of horse brasses and horse bells. He would sing long forgotten songs, learned from his father, such as 'The Farmer's Boy' and the lugubrious 'What is the Blood on thy Shirt Sleeve?' as he continued on his rounds. The antics of Billy Drabble, clay miner, also earned him the reputation as an eccentric. In the First World War Billy had sustained injuries from which he was never to fully recover. He was a familiar figure at the wheel of the family's steam wagon, thick black smoke billowing in its wake, but was prone to accost strangers, especially young lads, making them stand to attention and marching them up and down the street like soldiers!

In the days before mass entertainment games and sport played an important role in the lives of the valley people. Many of them were focussed on the local pubs. The Stannington Hunt, was one of the oldest in the country and met at any one of the pubs in the valley during the nineteenth and early twentieth centuries. Its records echo down the centuries to the time that these valleys provided sport for their medieval lords. In the years before the First World War the hunt regularly turned out to follow the dogs on foot, chasing hares for miles through the valley and over the local moors. The valley's clay miners would enjoy a game of knur and spell, a regular Yorkshire miners' pastime, on the fields behind the Royal in Dungworth and the Robin Hood had both a skittle alley and a rifle range. The Stannington Cricket Club is recorded playing in 1805, making it one of the earliest in the country. Each of the tiny villages in the valley had cricket and football teams that competed in local leagues.

Although it's a way of life that has been pretty much swept away, the feeling of belonging to a closely knit community is not entirely lost. The valley is still largely self-contained with its own primary schools at Dungworth, Loxley and Stannington. Its ancient church at High Bradfield, on the hillside above the bend of the river, looks over its enormous parish. The scatter of nonconformist chapels, most now converted into quirky though desirable dwellings, is reminiscent of one of the Welsh mining valleys, an illusion that is strengthened by both the heritage of mining and tradition of singing. The only shop within the valley beyond Loxley and Stannington is now the Old Post Office in Low Bradfield. The local pubs, The Royal at Dungworth, the Nag's Head at Stacy Bank, The Horns and The Plough at Bradfield, and the Strines however, attract numbers of visitors from the city.

The upper valley is secluded and tends to keep itself to itself. The historic farms that dot the landscape are generally hidden, reached only down long tractor-width tracks. Given the common experience of rural crime there's an understandable suspicion towards unrecognised visitors and to outsiders there's an unwelcoming air of 'Cold Comfort Farm' about the glimpsed dilapidation and apparently random pieces of incomprehensible farm machinery that lay rusting and abandoned. Beyond the creeping suburbanisation of Loxley and Stannington there are only isolated farmsteads, small clusters and hamlets, built from the dark gritstone extracted from local quarries, and only the twin settlements of High and Low Bradfield and Dungworth can aspire to be villages. Within the valley other tiny clusters at Ughill and Holdworth retain an ancient air and appear not to have developed since they were the only valley settlements listed in the Domesday Book, amongst the possessions of a Saxon called Alderne. The only other little grouping of cottages, farmsteads and former chapel at Storrs accommodated local miners, farmers and cutlers in the nineteenth century.

I don't want to give the impression that little has altered within the Loxley Valley over the centuries for that would be quite untrue. Even before the industrial revolution had got underway external forces were influencing the way of life of the valley dwellers. From early days the energy of the river had been harnessed with the building of water mills. By the eighteenth century a string of mills along the valley bottom rang with the metallic sounds of forging and rolling to shape steel into blades whose fine edges were ground on locally cut sandstone grindstones. Many of the farmers who had wrested a precarious living from the poor stony hillsides for generations would augment their sparse living by adding a smithy to their outbuildings and became outworkers of the Sheffield trades, forging blades and grinding them in the mills beside the river below, before finishing and hafting the completed knives in their workshops. Pack horse trails snaked through the valley bringing materials and returning with finished products to the masters in the town over the hill.

At the same time Sheffield's growing steel industry exerted a growing influence over the working lives of the valley dwellers. The local geology is such that thin seams of coal and fireclays outcrop on the hillsides, both vital to the city's developing industry. Thus, another tier was added to the local economy, that of mining, so that, over the next hundred years or so, this remarkable agricultural valley exhibited a unique economy based on water supply, coal and gannister mining, game-keeping, forestry, sheep and dairy farming and edge-tool production. And then, midway through the nineteenth century, the landscape of the valley was transformed by the construction of colossal embankments and the flooding of the valley floor to create four huge reservoirs serving the needs for water of the rapidly growing population of the city over the hill and leading to the event that would mark out the Loxley Valley in the history of world disasters.

The twentieth century saw a gradual stagnation and decline in this way of life. Although large areas of the upper valley had been turned over to commercial forestry after the First World War, much of the land continued to be farmed in much the same manner as in the past. Horses were still being used on the land and for local milk deliveries into the 1960s, but it was getting harder to make a living. The waterwheels, although their use had lingered on well into the second half of the nineteenth century, finally succumbed to steam powered technology, a handful of rural cutlers still managed to eke out a living as outworkers but were never replaced, the mines closed and, by the 1980s the brick kilns of the massive factories in the valley floor that produced refractory bricks from the local clay for the declining steel industry were cold. Acres of decaying sheds still stand derelict.

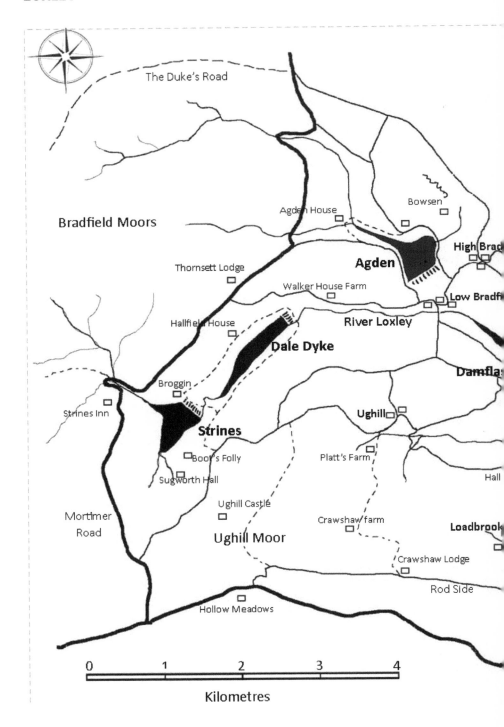

The Loxley Valley

Golden Plover

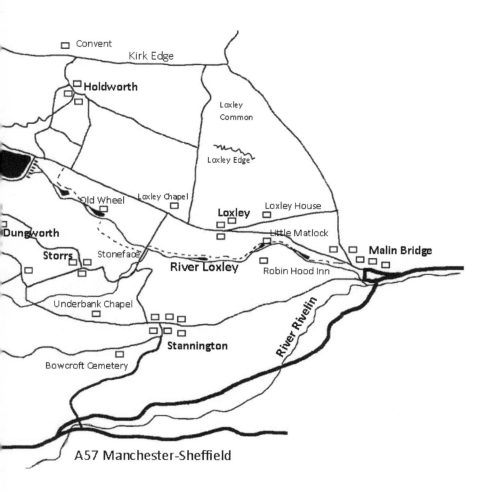

Developing Local Tensions

Dogged campaigners have, since the First World War, fought tooth and nail to retain the valley's rural character, but on both the northern and southern hillsides of the lower valley the residential suburbs of the city have encroached. By the mid-nineteenth century a ribbon development of houses had already crept from Malin Bridge, the settlement at the point at which the Rivelin and Loxley meet, to connect to the old settlement of Loxley but the residential development of the higher, steeper hillsides on the southern ridge between the Loxley and Rivelin valleys at Stannington came much later. The map of Stannington as recently as 1948 shows a very different pattern to the one we see today. Even then there was no nuclear village as such, it consisted of a number of small clusters; Knowle Top, Nethergate, Uppergate, Nook End and Town End. Interwar housing had spread along the main road up the hill but it was Sheffield's housing policy in 1962 that brought about a complete transformation of the village with the building of the Stannington council housing estate, including the three brutalist tower blocks that form such a feature of the skyline. At the same time many of the older farmhouses and buildings of Stannington were lost and the character of the village changed forever.

Today tensions are being felt in the valley. Heralded by the recent proposal for the development of a new housing scheme on a former industrial site beside the river in the valley bottom, the age-old pattern of settlement and Green Belt status is today under threat and highly contested. This is nothing new. In the 1980s a new estate, called the Acorn Estate, was laid out on the hillside sloping down the valley side from Stannington. In 2004 the Peak Park Policy Committee issued a Design Statement that summed up local feelings on the development:

> Local people feel the Acorn estate is an example of how <u>not</u> to design housing for the Loxley Valley. It was built in the early nineteen eighties, despite opposition from many local people. They still resent the way it dominates the top of the hill even though the builders attempted to produce local character by using stone, and copied traditional features from local barns and farm buildings. Even so, Acorn Hill still gives the impression of a sprawling suburban estate, lacking local character and completely out of keeping with its surroundings. Its flaws are in layout and density, and in the lack of a vegetation strategy.

Thirty or so years on, the new houses of the Acorn Estate have to a large extent melded into the landscape, screened by the maturing trees, but it is doubtful that any new such scheme to develop housing on a greenfield site in the valley would gain approval. There are, however, a number of 'brownfield' sites, in particular the huge derelict brick factory sites, for which housing presents one solution to their redevelopment. As I write, the final homes on a new estate of sixty-two houses, called unimaginatively 'The Brickworks', that have been built on the former site of Dyson's refractory brick works are being advertised for sale at prices from £299,950 to a staggering £619,950! The site, which stands in open country on a hillside called 'The Griffs', between Stannington and Dungworth, had been derelict since 2006 and plans for its development by Wakefield-based housebuilder Avant Homes, which finally gained planning consent in April 2017, were controversial. *"We think market housing would be an inappropriate use of this site,"* said the Friends of the Peak District and Council for the Preservation of Rural England, the CPRE, on learning of the proposals and continued;

> Just because a Green Belt site is disused and in need of cleaning up doesn't make it suitable for housing, and certainly not for a generic housing solution from a volume housebuilder. We believe this is, without doubt, the wrong development for the site. The illustrated 'quasi-traditional' style street scenes suggest a pattern book residential estate

with token green space and the sad-looking stump of the old landmark Dyson chimney. It looks like the kind of pastiche nonsense that gives development a bad reputation and suburbanises the countryside.

Prior to the commencement of building the developers tried to be reassuring; *"The 12 acre site represents the first incursion into the Sheffield green belt and as such was required to deliver a housing scheme of exemplar design and sustainability credentials, ensuring the 62 homes built on the site will be of the highest quality."* Now that it's built people will have their own opinions as to the appropriateness of the development in this rural context and whether the developers have successfully met their own brief.

Now the battlelines have been drawn up once again. Residents of the valley are bracing themselves for what could be a bitter fight against the development of a 'township' of 300 new homes in the middle of the green belt in woodland beside the river, a site presently occupied by derelict brick factory buildings. Hundreds of objectors have already made their views known to the planners claiming the development would ruin the ancient woodland, destroy wildlife, cause traffic chaos and be dangerous as the land is prone to flooding. It's clear to everyone that something must be done to clear the dangerous and unsightly ruins that have been scandalously abandoned by the former owners, but who pays for the clear up and who has the final say in the site's future is contentious.

Chroniclers of the Valley's Story

In researching the curiosities of the Loxley Valley I've been struck by how many people have published their own thoughts on the subject. The earliest of these was Mr John Wilson, who occupied nearby Broomhead Hall during much of the 18th century. Broomhead Hall was a grand Victorian pile, mainly used as a shooting lodge, that stood hard against bleak moorland just over the ridge to the north of Bradfield. The original house was built in 1640 by Christopher Wilson, who is remembered for having turned down the chance of a knighthood by declining his invitation to the Coronation of Charles I. This hall stood on the site of a far earlier hall of the Wilsons who had occupied it from the thirteenth century. It was, however, destroyed by fire and rebuilt in 1831 and this in turn was tragically demolished in 1980, leaving only a few surviving outbuildings.

John Wilson was typical of his time, a Georgian landed gentleman who had the leisure and wealth to occupy himself entirely to antiquarian research and collecting. It is said that he had *"a little museum consisting of rare prints, a few paintings, and other objects natural and artificial, ancient and modern, of different degrees of curiosity and value and a cabinet of coins of considerable value."* A veritable local cabinet of curiosities. I can well imagine the ancient, dark wood-panelled hall, dusty bookshelves filled with leather-bound books, and manuscripts lining every wall, candlelight glinting from the glass covered cabinets of Bronze Age and Roman artefacts that were occasionally turned up by the plough in his fields.

He would also collect local tales, customs and traditions from folk of the neighbourhood, a delightful example of such a local tale that he relates is:

1780, Joseph Hadfield of Wigtwizzle, aged 55, tells the story of
a man who was rescued after falling 40 fathoms down a mine shaft.
Within a week he died after falling off a three legged-stool.

But, above all, it is to him that we owe thanks for amassing an enormous collection of original deeds, court rolls, manorial records, and other material, dating from the thirteenth century onwards, relating to the locality, many to the Loxley Valley. Wilson's archive went into private hands but much of it was eventually recovered and compiled by Mr J.G. Ronksley of Sheffield and was bought by Sheffield Libraries in 1916. It is now an invaluable resource for local historians in Sheffield Archives.

Joseph Hunter, in preparing '*Hallamshire, The History and Topography of the Parish of Sheffield in the County of York*', the definitive work on the history of Sheffield, published in 1819, visited Broomhead Hall and acknowledged the work done by John Wilson. He was able to consult Wilson's manuscript collection and *Hallamshire* includes the research he carried out into the pedigree of many of the families of Sheffield and the surrounding area. Hunter was a Unitarian Minister, antiquarian, and deputy keeper of public records for England. He was acknowledged to be one of the leading historians of the time and became Vice President of the Society of Antiquaries of London. Amongst his many publications is a pamphlet he published in 1852 on Robin Hood, in which he argued that a servant of this name at the court of Edward II was identical with the famous outlaw. More of which later. In 1912 a group met at Sheffield University and created the Hunter Archaeological Society in his memory, which is still the city's foremost archaeological research body. One of the founders of the Society was GHB Ward, who in 1901 founded the Sheffield Clarion Ramblers that was instrumental in researching rights of way and organising mass campaigns such as the Kinder Mass Trespass and the mass trespass along the Duke's Road across the Bradfield Moors in 1932 to assert these lost rights to roam.

From 1839 until his death in 1903, Rev. Alfred Gatty, was the much loved and respected vicar of Ecclesfield, the huge parish that until the mid-nineteenth century included the Loxley Valley. Although both he and his wife, Margaret, were literary figures of considerable note it was Margaret who achieved lasting fame as the author of *Aunt Judy's Children's Magazine* and illustrator of the standard work on British seaweeds. In 1869 Alfred enlarged and updated Joseph Hunter's *Hallamshire* and this is the valuable edition that has been my constant guide in researching the valley's story. Amongst his own works on local subjects, he published *Sheffield, Past and Present* in 1873 and *A Life at One Living* in 1884.

It was, however, not an academic or historian but the reporter and proprietor of the *Sheffield Times* weekly newspaper, Samuel Harrison, who, in 1864, was to produce the most vivid and evocative description of the valley. In *A Complete History of the Great Flood at Sheffield*, he gives us a snapshot of its people, their occupations and buildings at one tumultuous moment in time; providing a constant reference point throughout this book.

Amongst other prolific authors and collectors of local subjects Sidney Oldall Addy, stands out. He came from Norton and was the author of a number of books on local folklore and history, his best-known being *The Hall of Waltheof*, subtitled *The Early Condition and Settlement of Hallamshire*, published in 1893. The many illustrations and engravings make this one of the most beautifully produced books ever published on Sheffield.

In recent years it has been David Hey, Emeritus Professor of Local and Family History at the University of Sheffield and President of the British Association for Local History, who has led the field in promoting the interest in local studies both locally and nationally. His researches, particularly into family history, made him a very popular speaker and writer and he has many publications to his name, his last works being *Historic Hallamshire, A History of the Peak District Moors* and *The South Yorkshire Countryside*, all of which have been invaluable in compiling this book. Very sadly David died in 2016.

2

High Bradfield and the Lords of the Chase

A place that God began but never finished.

SYDNEY ADDY

July 6th, 2014 Le Grand Depart

It's a big day for the valley, almost certainly the biggest that there has ever been, a beautiful summer's day, and thousands of people have flocked here to the tiny village of High Bradfield from far and wide. Many have camped overnight in the fields in the temporary campsites quickly set up by local farmers, that give a fairground air with flags and food stalls. 'The World Looks to us This Weekend' proclaims the headline in the *Yorkshire Post*. Incredibly, one of the greatest spectacles in the world's sporting calendar is scheduled to take place here this morning; Day 2 of the Tour de France; Yorkshire is hosting 'Le Grand Depart'. This major event has caught the public imagination. Flocks of yellow-dyed sheep stand out on the hillsides of the Dales and thousands of decorated yellow bikes mark the route. This second stage, York to Sheffield, is classed as a 'Medium Mountain Stage' of 201 km. Disappointingly a crash in the sprint in Harrogate at the end of Day 1 has caused Mark Cavendish, the firm favourite of the Yorkshire supporters and tipped to win this year, to fall and he will not start Stage 2, so there's no chance of a glimpse of him this morning.

To join the colourful throngs of people lining the narrow roads I've walked across the valley from Dungworth. Whether by lucky chance or design the local roads of the Loxley Valley have been the first to receive attention under a city-wide initiative to remedy the atrocious state of Sheffield's roads and have been completely resurfaced. The new, smooth grey surface of the route has been adorned with chalk slogans and words of encouragement to the riders who will swoop down from the north, through High Bradfield and immediately turn tight left up Kirk Edge Road, a 20% gradient for 800 metres, renamed for the event 'Le Côte de Bradfield'. I settle to wait with the family at a vantage point at the top of the climb, 100 vertical metres above the village. Helicopters circle overhead, police motorbikes skim past and flags of all colours and nationalities are waved.

The crowds grow, spilling from the verges into the roadway. Anticipation rises to a crescendo as motorcycle outriders herald the approach of the riders. Caught up in the excitement I cheer wildly, as suddenly the multicoloured peloton surges up the hill towards us and disappears along the ridge, closely followed by a cavalcade of support cars.

I hadn't anticipated the speed that these elite athletes would fly up the step gradient. *"It was all a bit of a blur,"* reported the Yorkshire Post the next day. *"In a whirl of Lycra and straining calf muscles, the sleek, bent bodies flashed past, urged on by the crowds. The spectators pressed forward, to within inches of the wheels in places. It was anarchic and furious. It was the Tour."* For most of those who had waited patiently along the route the brief glimpse of the riders had been worth the wait. *"I was here since 7am and just heard sirens and it was over so fast,"* said Daniel McKenzie from Darlington. *"It was exciting,"* he said, *"but maybe I'd have seen more on the telly."* It was a colourful pageant, all over in no time. The crowds began to disperse and the village returned to its usual somnolent peace and quiet. Stage 2, incidentally, was won by Italy's Vincenzo Nibali, the ultimate race winner.

Since 'Le Tour' the valley has become a magnet for weekend cyclists of all abilities, but the steeper hills have a particular attraction for the keen club members. 'The Bradfield Hill Climb,' up Woodfall Lane, from Low Bradfield up to High Bradfield, is particularly favoured by local clubs and is a regular fixture on their calendars. It's less than half a mile but the steep gradient of the 300 ft climb, the narrowness of the road and the tight bends present a suitably gruelling challenge to sort the men from the boys in the cycling world. In 2016 Calum Brown of the 'Cycles in Motion' club set a remarkable new course record of 1 minute 58.3 seconds to complete the climb, a feat of strength and endurance that I find incredible! My son, Adam, a very keen club cyclist, has done it in 2 minutes 44 seconds.

December 14th 2019 High Bradfield Church

I close the gate and enter the graveyard of Bradfield Churchyard high on the hillside overlooking Agden Reservoir and pause to take in the incomparable view across the valley towards the far western moorlands. December is an appropriate month to visit this majestic church as it is dedicated to St Nicholas, an unusual dedication. Being the patron saint of fishermen, his churches are more generally found on the coast. The little village that extends from the church gates is scarcely more than a pub, a scatter of farm buildings and a few cottages, but its church, standing aside from the other buildings above the sheep grazing hillside and set amongst serried ranks of gravestones, is magnificent, curiously out of place in such a tiny settlement, a stately, solitary building, framed by the filigree silhouettes of winter beeches and oaks, with pinnacles and battlemented tower. The pale greenish, grey-fawn colour of its local gritstone masonry matches exactly that of the gravestones and the surrounding dry-stone field walls. The windows are enormous, tall and pointed; each one divided into three by vertical stone mullions in the style termed 'Gothic Perpendicular', giving a clue to its fifteenth-century rebuilding. Most of the downspouts from the roof emerge from the gaping mouths of crudely fashioned gargoyles but the eastern corners facing the village are decorated with two most curious stone effigies. One is a scaly-winged horned dragon with gaping jaws, whilst at the other corner sits a dog, uncomfortably perched on the sloping top of the corner buttress, peering into the distant horizon. They appear to serve no function other than decorative. I can't help smiling irreverently as I realise that the dog reminds me of Gromit!

Bradfield sits at the heart of the valley. In effect it's two villages three quarters of a kilometre apart in distance and almost a hundred metres apart in height. They are known rather unimaginatively as 'Low Bradfield' and 'High Bradfield'. In the earliest medieval documents that survive the upper settlement is called not Bradfield but 'Kirkton', clearly referencing an earlier church. Although the settlement almost certainly existed at the time, the Domesday Book of 1086 has no mention of it, unlike the far smaller nearby hamlets of Ughill and Holdworth. It may well be that Bradfield was one of the sixteen 'berewicks', the name given to small settlements, in Hallamshire that the Domesday enumerator bothered to count but not to name! In the later 1100s it was referred to in Papal documents as 'Bradefeld', which would be at about the time when William de Lovetot, the first Norman Lord of Hallamshire, the early name for the Sheffield area, built the Church of St.

Mary, Ecclesfield, nine kilometres to the east. It seems probable that the original church of St Nicholas, here in Bradfield, was built around the same time to serve the needs of this huge rural area, not as a parish church with its own priest, but as a chapel of ease of Ecclesfield, a curious status that it was to retain throughout the centuries until the mid-nineteenth century. The eighteenth-century antiquarian John Wilson of nearby Broomhead Hall claimed to have found evidence in one of the medieval windows, since destroyed, that the original building had been erected in 1109, which seems plausible as the 'Chapelry of Bradfield' is named in a grant made to the Canons of Worksop by the new Lord of the Manor of Hallamshire, Gerard de Furnival, at the end of the twelfth century. Few signs of this Norman church survive, for the impressive building we see today dates from a complete remodelling in the 'Gothic Perpendicular' style in about 1480.

Bodysnatchers!

Here, to the right of the iron gates into the graveyard, stands a most curious building. It looks like a tall, narrow tollhouse, battlemented to match the church, with lancet windows on three sides facing different directions. It reminds me of one of the toll-houses built in the eighteenth century along the turnpike roads and this design unmistakably proclaims the purpose; it's a watch-house, one of only a few in the country and the only one in Yorkshire.

It turns out that the alarm that occasioned the building of this watch-house in 1831 was not altogether misplaced. The building's story is linked to a very highly regarded Sheffield surgeon, Dr Hall Overend, who had begun teaching medical students in Sheffield from about 1811 and established an anatomy museum at his home in Church Street in the town centre, where he conducted demonstrations of dissection on dead bodies. There was a problem, however, in that, before the Anatomy Act of 1832 the only legal supply of corpses for anatomical purposes like this were those of people condemned to death and their bodies used for dissection. By the early nineteenth century, as sentencing and punishments were gradually becoming more humane, only about 56 people a year in the whole country were unfortunate enough to be condemned to such treatment, nothing like the number required by the new medical schools. This gave rise to the gruesome practice of employing 'Resurrection Men', the most celebrated being Edinburgh's renowned Burke and Hare, to disinter recently buried bodies. It was said that Hall Overend carried out his duty of acquiring subjects on which to demonstrate *"with vigour and success."* Not that Overend was personally responsible for the grisly night time exploits that caused such distress in remote village graveyards, but it was said that he was more than aware of what was afoot when his students were involved in planning the clandestine operations, keeping watch and carrying away bodies. In order to escape detection it is said that they would dress the body in a cloak and hat, sit it upright between two students in a gig, and drive from the graveyard to the town centre! There is even a tale that on one occasion Overend was alarmed when disturbed by the town constables, having hidden a body in his house in Church Street opposite Sheffield Parish Church. It is probably not surprising that Bradfield churchyard, in such an isolated spot, should attract the unwelcome attention of these gruesome Sheffield 'resurrectionists', and in the year 1830 they got wind of the fact that a young man in the Bradfield area had died of consumption and was duly buried in the churchyard close to the east end of the church. They accordingly made plans to remove the body. All went to plan until a person living near the church, hearing a gig and the sound of horses' hooves pacing about in the dark cobbled street, looked out to see what was amiss. The alarm was raised and the men in the gig hightailed it back down the valley. One of the perpetrators however, was abandoned in the churchyard and was unable, because of deep snow, to make a swift getaway. He was apprehended, tried, and sentenced to twelve month's imprisonment. It seems that it was shortly after this event that the watch-house was built. Today the building is the most curious dwelling house in the district.

Stories in Stone

Passing through the wrought iron gates into the graveyard, rank upon rank of rounded headstones surround the church on all sides. Close to the church, set into the paving, are the oldest, a group of unusually early slabs, dating, like the memorial to Nicholas Steade that I'm standing on, from 1651. The gravestone to 'Sarah, ye first wife of Anthony Wood June 9th 1678 & also Mary his second wife May 16th 1685', on which the mason has allowed himself free reign to indulge a talent for fancy script and wonderfully curlicued capitals, lies close by. Other families, whose names are still familiar in the valley, are memorialised in similar 300-year-old stones; the Trickets, Ibbotsons, Drabbles, Shaws, Hagues; families that still farm the hillsides today.

Further on, amidst the generally uniform rows of nineteenth century burials, I discover with delight the curiously carved headstone that marks the final resting place of George Hammerton of Sugworth who died in 1874. It is one of the most curious memorials that I have ever seen. It leaves us in no doubt as to his occupation in life for at the head of the rounded stone is depicted a fat, woolly sheep, or ram since it has fine curly horns. It sits comfortably on a table (or is it an altar?) complacently staring out forever with wide, round eyes. In front of him a pair of sheep shears have been carved, the exact pattern that were, and still are, made by the Burgon and Ball tool company of Malin Bridge, just down the valley. To emphasise the local connection, behind the sheep rise the curved timbers of a local cruck-built barn. It's a unique piece of local art and craftsmanship and I love it. But that's not quite all, for the stone also has a most curious verse that explains the sheep analogy;

Jesu thy wandering sheep behold,
See Lord, with yearning bowels see,
The souls that cannot find the fold,
Till sought and gatherer'd in by thee.

I can't imagine that there can be many grave memorials that mention 'bowels!

Amongst the hundreds of names on the grave stones many are quaint and charming. Alongside the path, almost hidden in the long grass, are Nicodemus Bramall and his wife Annis of Agden House. The Bramalls are a well-established local family who still farm nearby in Dungworth. In another part of the graveyard lies the body of Henry Bramall, who, the census records tell us, was a well-to-do Bradfield farmer of twenty-seven acres and also a file manufacturer employing nine men and two boys. We learn more about Henry from a report in the *Yorkshire Post* on Wednesday 10th March 1886 that records his death. Tragically, he had been discovered in the early hours of the previous night by two of his sons, hanging from a kitchen beam. In a handwritten suicide note he made reference to grave allegations made against him by his second wife Jane, to whom he had been unhappily married for over twenty years.

During the inquest that followed, the jury heard that Henry had been *"perpetually tantalized"* by allegations that were *"thrown at him by his wife"* of being over-familiar with his teenage daughter Mary Eliza. It was to become clear, however, that there was no foundation to this whatsoever. Even his wife and daughter stated that this was the case, and evidence soon emerged suggesting that his wife Jane had a severe personality disorder. Whilst the newspaper reports were entitled 'Suicide of a Sheffield Manufacturer and Merchant' the inquest verdict delivered by the jury was not one of suicide; it was an open verdict. The reason for this somewhat perplexing decision may well be that if Henry's death had been suicide he would not have been able to be buried here in the consecrated ground surrounding the church. So Henry was afforded a full Christian burial in his local churchyard as the church records show.

But if the story of Henry Bramall is a sad one it pales when compared with the events that overtook the subsequent generations of his family, events that could comfortably grace the pages of one of the more lurid Victorian Gothic horror novels. We only have to peruse the inscriptions on the gravestones here to begin to understand what misery many families went through in the nineteenth century in losing children to early death, but the account of what happened to the family of Henry Bramall's son William and his wife Clara is a tale of unimaginable grief, for she was to suffer the fate of having to bury her husband and every one of her nine children before she died at the age of eighty-nine at Sheffield's City General Hospital. What makes this even more tragic and unusual is that three of her daughters committed suicide by drowning.

The couple's first three children Catherine, Alfred and Mary died as children, all in the two years of 1893–94. Clara subsequently gave birth to three daughters, Ernestine, Georgina and Gladys, and then three more Frank,

Maggie and Clara who tragically died as children. Only the three daughters survived to their teens but in 1915 disaster was to strike the family again.

At this time they were living at Wadsley, up the hill from Loxley. A newspaper report from 29th March 1915, under the headline 'Drowning Mystery', reports the death of their middle daughter, eighteen-year-old Georgina, who had been missing from home since 5th January. She had been seen wandering along the road beside Damflask Reservoir on the afternoon after having taken her father his lunch, but what happened after that remains a mystery. There was no indication that it was suicide and whilst foul play may have been a possibility, the length of time the body had been submerged in the water would have made such a conclusion speculative to say the least, and so an open verdict by the inquest jury was the only option.

Her father William died in 1926 and so it left Clara and her two remaining daughters, neither of whom married. The next tragic reference to the family occurs in a probate record for the eldest daughter, Ernestine, then aged 52, which states that *"This woman committed suicide in the pond in Hillsborough Park on 27th August 1947."* A handwritten note adds the words *"The Coroner's verdict was suicide"* but as it did not say *"whilst this woman was of unsound mind"* there was no service in church and the prayer book service was not used, a pretty harsh and unfeeling attitude we might think, especially considering her mother's history. But worse was yet to come. Four months later, in January 1948, forty-nine year old Gladys, the last of Clara's children, was interred. A stark note in the register says, *"Drowned herself, as did her sister"* but it adds, *"but the verdict was such that we were able to have the first part of the service in church."* Let's hope that Clara was able to find some small consolation from this. She had outlived all the nine children she gave birth to. Six died in childhood and three drowned. Two were deemed suicide by the coroner and the other remains a mystery. The last Bramall entry in the Burial record of St Nicholas Church is Clara herself. She died of grief and old age.

The inscriptions on one or two of the headstones catch my particular attention, for they record specific events. Just above the church stands a group that commemorate various members of the Trickett family of Malin Bridge. One of them is more elaborately carved than the others and marks the resting place of James and Elizabeth Trickett and their three children, Jemima, James and George, who, the inscription tells us, were all carried away and drowned in the 'Great Flood' on the night of March 11th 1864. Below the names is inscribed the following verse of typical lugubrious Victorian doggerel;

Whoe'er may be blamed for the recent distress,
Our duty to God it makes none the less;
Whate'er be the fault this, this is most true,
The flood is a warning to me and to you.

-which seems a pretty harsh way to remember a family that did nothing to deserve such an appalling fate!

Above the church stands the headstone of Samuel Hammerton. It reads, *"Samuel Hammerton of Walker House, Nr. Bradfield, who was killed on the return journey from Chester Fair, July 5th 1871, aged 44 years."* As it happens we know something of Samuel, for he played a small part in the story of the night of the Great Flood. He was a farmer at Walker House Farm that still stands on Dale Road opposite the Dale Dyke Reservoir embankment and it is recorded that, at about seven o'clock on the fateful evening of Friday, March 11th 1864, he was the first to alert the contractors, who had almost completed the building of the dam wall, to the imminent danger posed by the fissure that had opened in the embankment which was to cause such devastation later that night. Whilst he avoided the fate of so many of neighbours on that terrible night he was to meet his fate in unusual circumstances seven years later. A newspaper article of July 7th 1871 recorded the circumstances of his curious death. He and a companion, Joseph Birley of nearby Thornsett House farm, had travelled to the country fair at Chester to purchase cattle and were returning home in the brake van of the train in which the cattle were being transported. Near Sandbach, in the process of shunting to allow the down mail to pass, the van and five wagons jumped the rails. Both men were violently thrown out and killed.

November 2008, Bradfield Castle

Following the footpath through the churchyard, being careful to close the gates to avoid allowing the over-friendly grass-trimming sheep to escape, I pass through the gate into the steeply sloping wood on the other side. To the left the ground drops precipitously down to the grey water of Agden Reservoir, glimpsed through the trees. To my right the narrow footpath leads up into a wide-open space, enclosed on one side by the cliff edge and on the other by a massive crescent-shaped embankment about 30 feet high and 100 yards long. Ahead, across the clearing, at the far end of the embankment, stands a startlingly prominent feature, a conical wooded hill, 60 feet high, encircled by a deep and wide ditch. Squirrels scurry along the bare silvery branches of the beech and oak trees that grow on the huge mound and parties of tits flit and flutter, like mechanical toys, amongst the thick carpet of leaf litter. There's not a soul in sight. From where I stand here in the clearing the mound is rounded, shaped rather like a Christmas pudding (it's even got a holly tree growing near the top) but viewed from the outer side of the embankment it's an almost perfect cone. The whole feature might well have come from a children's history book illustration of a Norman motte and bailey castle, and accordingly it is known as 'Bailey Hill'. The whole site was purchased a couple of years ago by one of the country's most eminent folk singers and musicians who lives down in the valley. It already has an appropriate, slightly hippy atmosphere and maybe this ancient gathering place will see folky gatherings in the future; music and song and possibly woodland marriages with fairy lights. I hope so. It's a magical spot that must have been well frequented at some stage in the remote past. Now, however, this amazing site is largely forgotten and somewhat forlorn. Antiquarians would refer to such features as these as 'earthworks', a catch-all term referring to features whose story is pretty much unrecorded, which certainly fits the case here at Bradfield.

It seems curious in the extreme that such a monumental structure as here at Bailey Hill should have left no trace in the historical record. Commentators have, in aiming to make sense of the mysterious earthworks at various times, fallen back on conjecture, educated guesswork or sheer speculation in attempts to explain the origin of these features. The earliest of the antiquarian visitors to the site was the Rev. John Wilson of nearby Broomhead Hall who, in an address to the Society of Antiquaries in 1779, pronounced it to have been *"a station of the Danes"* whilst Joseph Hunter in 1826 was firm in his opinion that *"Bailey Hill is a Saxon camp, as fair and perfect as when first constructed, save that the keep is overgrown with bushes."* Sydney Addy, a third antiquarian visitor to the site, included a whole chapter in his beautifully produced *The Hall of Waltheof*, published in 1893, complete with plans and drawings. His conclusion was unequivocal. *"The evidence which I shall give will point to the conclusion that Bailey Hill was the place of the village assembly,"* he asserts, dismissing the idea that it was any kind of fortification. He then gives a rambling discourse on the supposed customs of 'The Norsemen', saying:

> If we may apply the customs of the Norsemen to this village situate
> in the Danish part of England we may infer that near to the house of
> the village chieftain was the seat whereupon he administered justice
> or gave advice, the place where the people met both to worship and
> to deliberate in council

giving the close proximity to the church as supporting evidence.

Despite such conjectures the structures are today regarded as having been constructed by the Normans, for it is clear that prior to the invasion led by William the Conqueror castles in England were few and far between. The late Professor David Hey of Sheffield University, and one of the country's most respected local historians, concluded that there was no doubt that Bailey Hill is a motte-and-bailey castle calling it *"one of the best preserved and most dramatic motte-and-baileys in Yorkshire."* If so the structure harks back to the early days following the Norman invasion of the eleventh century, when our area was known as 'Hallamshire', one of those curious Saxon 'shires-within-a-shire' focussed on the ancient Parish of Ecclesfield with its two daughter parishes of Sheffield and Bradfield. At the time of the invasion Hallamshire was part of the demesne of Waltheof, the powerful Saxon Earl of Huntington, but following his execution for taking part in a rebellion against William I, it became part of the extensive South Yorkshire holdings of Roger de Busli, holder of the Honour of Tickhill. As such Bailey Hill would have been right at the north western extremity of his possessions, a possibly vulnerable corner. Knowing the fondness of Norman barons for constructing such fortresses to subdue the native population it seems probable that our earthworks here dates from the turbulent times of Roger or his successors, the Lovetots who built the first wooden castle down in Sheffield during the twelfth century.

We have a clue in the Bayeux Tapestry as to how this unlikely construction might have worked. Into the tapestry is woven the depiction of an attack on the moated hillock of Dinant in Normandy showing a hill, shaped very much like the one at Bradfield, on top of which was constructed a platform on cantilevered supports which was wide enough to support a small wooden building, a sort of watchtower that could be used as a defensive refuge in times of danger, approached by a ramp. At Bradfield could the ramp have been built across from the end of the crescent shaped embankment? It seems possible.

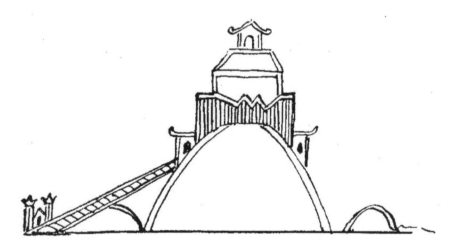

If we know little about the story of Bailey Hill we know even less about what is marked on the OS map in gothic script as 'Castle' in a field at the other side of the village. On the opposite side of the road to the Bradfield Brewery the hillside is marked with slight ditches and embankments that could or could not indicate an ancient site, but that, for what it's worth, is all we know.

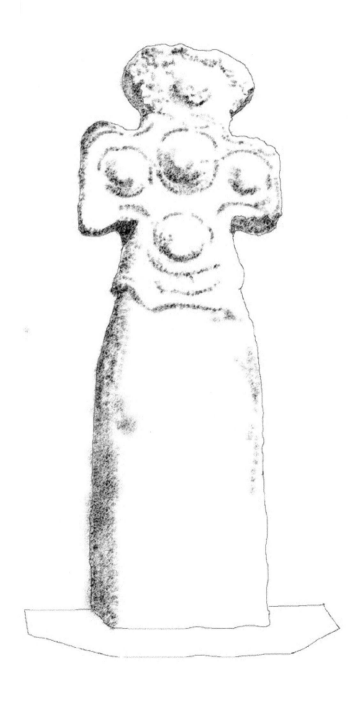

The Medieval Church

The interior of St Nicholas is huge, although whether it is large enough to accommodate the 1141 communicants that church records tell us attended on Easter Day 1617 I would doubt. Whereas the stone outside has been darkened by centuries of weather to a dark, mossy grey, the stone of the pillars and walls inside the building has retained the original warm honey colour. Most of the pillars carrying the four tall, pointed arches on each side of the nave, are octagonal in section, in the 'perpendicular' style, though a couple are round; clearly remnants of an earlier Norman building. Features like this make exploring old churches so fascinating. They invariably retain features that chronicle their own story and frequently, like this church, house clues to the history of the community.

The first of these clues that I spot is a very unusual stone cross that stands about five feet tall beside the north wall. It is said to have been unearthed down the hill in Low Bradfield in 1870, and placed here in the church in 1883. There is a local legend that the cross marked the spot in the valley that was chosen to build the church but that as soon as building was started the work done during the day was transported by supernatural forces up the hill to the present site. It's a story that re-emerges elsewhere when there was a disagreement about where to build the church, and certainly it would appear to have made greater sense to build it on the site now occupied by the cricket field in the centre of Low Bradfield than hundreds of feet up the hill. It is by far the most curious artefact in the valley and, as an inveterate collector of curios, I'm becoming obsessed by it.

Almost nothing is known for certain about the cross. It is generally dismissed in a couple of sentences as '*A Saxon or Celtic cross, possibly a wayside marker or boundary stone.*' What is certain is that the design is like no other cross in our region, of which there are several. The Saxon crosses from Sheffield, as well as Eyam, Bakewell and Bradbourne in the nearby Peak District, bear elaborate and sophisticated designs of vine scrolls and both pagan and Christian symbols. If not executed by the same hand they appear to have emanated from the same workshop or tradition of Mercian craftsmanship. The Bradfield cross is crude by comparison, with a rounded boss at the centre of the four arms of a cross, each of which bears a slightly smaller boss like half a tennis ball. The Celtic crosses of Ireland and Scotland have a similar design although these almost invariably have a circle around the arms. These designs have been suggested to hark back to pagan themes of cycles of the sun at the centre and the seasons or times of the day around it. In a rural area like the valley, where agriculture would have been marginal and entirely dependent on the weather, this makes sense to me. Crosses of a similar style have been unearthed, or discovered built into the fabric of churches, further north in Yorkshire. Burnsall church, in Wharfedale, contains a cross with a strikingly similar head, and another at Middleton-on-the-Wolds bears the depiction of a Viking warrior on the shaft. It is thought that they give evidence of the wave of settlers of Norwegian descent who moved from the west, originally from Ireland, via Cumbria, early in the tenth century. Certain place names in our valley, as well as the cross itself, would suggest that these people settled here. The cross may or may not bear witness to a local Christian community. During this time there was a somewhat ambivalent attitude to religion, the Norsemen gradually embracing Christianity whilst retaining some of their old beliefs. There is the possibility that it may have been the grave marker of a local chief or headman, although the possibility of it being a boundary marker cannot be dismissed, Hallamshire having been on the border between the Anglo-Saxon kingdoms of Northumbria and Mercia. Our valley has been border country throughout ancient history.

In the opposite corner of the church two very curious faceless effigies catch my attention. Unlike the familiar stone statues that often commemorate fallen warriors in old churches these are woven from thin brown willow wands and clearly depict soldiers of the First World War, their only decoration being a red poppy on each chest. One sits wearily on the ancient parish chest whilst the other stands apparently on guard beside him, rifle at the ready. They are intricately modelled with helmets, belts and pouches. They were constructed by children at Dungworth Primary School as part of a very special project. During 2016 the local community took to heart the call for commemorations to honour the dead of the two great wars of the 20th century. The Dungworth, Bradfield and District Heritage Group set about researching the story of men and women from the valley who had played a part in the conflicts and discovered that the names of two local men who had lost their lives, Alan Charlesworth and Arthur Wingfield, had been missed from the Roll of Honour in the church. This touched a local nerve and stimulated an outpouring of support for the project. Two beautifully produced little books were published on 'The Forgotten Heroes' of the parish, the woven willow soldiers were installed in the church and the whole project culminated in a week-long celebration in October 2016 with a memorial trail, search lights beaming across the valley from World War Two battery sites and a service at which the focal point of the proceedings was the switch-on of the stunning light installation in which the outside of the church was suddenly illuminated by a field of bright red poppies that shone out across the valley, a spectacular and unforgettable event that was covered by press and TV.

The Talbot Lords of the Valley

Although there are clues in the fabric to suggest that a church was built close to Bailey Hill by the Normans, the perpendicular church of St Nicholas, that I'm enjoying visiting today, dates from a virtually complete rebuilding in the 1480s. I'm on the lookout for clues to who was responsible for creating such an extravagant building in the fifteenth century. The size and opulence of the building points to it being someone of wealth and power and the stone dog sitting up there so alert, with a collar around his neck, is the first clue to who this might be.

Inside the church I discover an emblem that I'm familiar with. It's in a window in the nave that is made up of pieces of glass recovered from the original medieval windows during the nineteenth century 'restoration'. It's a depiction of a golden lion standing with its paws raised, the crest of the Talbot family, the Earls of Shrewsbury, lords of the Manor of Hallamshire throughout the fifteenth and sixteenth centuries. The particular family member during the 1480s, when the present church was being built, was George Talbot, the 4th Earl, and to see his likeness you need only travel to Sheffield Cathedral for there on his memorial tomb lays his marble effigy, between his two wives, in the Shrewsbury Chapel, which he built. He was certainly a man of great power and wealth, a distinguished warrior under Henry VII and an honoured statesman under Henry VIII. It was he who built the first part of the Manor Lodge in the middle of the great Sheffield Deer Park and who, in 1530, had the 'honour' of entertaining Cardinal Wolsey there. I soon spot evidence that it was partly his love of hunting that prompted his interest in the Loxley Valley for, in the same window, is a depiction of a stag.

39

Looking upwards I can see that the joints between the dark oak roof timbers are decorated with carved bosses but they are a long way up and it's rather dark so I lay down on my back to photograph them with a telephoto lens. If the elderly couple of visitors who enter at that moment are surprised they are polite enough not to mention it. They have come over from Halifax to look round the church and have lunch at the 'Horns' next door. The camera reveals more than I dared hope. Amongst the dozen roof bosses there is a carved 'Green Man', the medieval emblem of new life and virility, his tongue stuck out in a profane gesture to the worshipers below, a couple of deer, two hunting dogs, a long-beaked bird and an animal that looks like an otter. In pride of place, however, over the chancel arch is placed a crude carving of a Talbot, his teeth bared, just like the one outside. These hunting dogs, massive deerhounds, were the emblem of the Talbot family, being a play on their name, reflecting their passion for the chase. The dog on the roof outside is the same breed. Here is clear proof of the association between the noble lords of Hallamshire and the valley.

In Medieval times the hunting rights across the Rivelin and Loxley valleys were enjoyed by the lords of Hallamshire; the Lovetots in the twelfth century, the Furnivals during the following two centuries and the Talbot, Earls of Shrewsbury, during the fifteenth and sixteenth centuries. As early as 1281 Thomas de Furnival, who had recently rebuilt Sheffield Castle in stone, in answering a crown enquiry into his rights and privileges, asserted that his ancestors had enjoyed the right to hunt within the lordship since the Norman Conquest. Across the Loxley and Rivelin valleys the lords designated three huge areas as 'chases' or 'friths' in which to enjoy the pleasures of the hunt. The largest of these areas was Rivelin Chase which encompassed the

Rivelin Valley and stretched across the Hallam Moors to Stanage. Most of the township of Stannington lay within this chase. The second chase, Hawksworth Frith, covered much of the moorland at the head of Bradfield Dale, which still retained the name into the seventeenth century, and gave rise to a local surname, whilst a third chase, known as Loxley Chase, encompassed the north side of the Loxley Valley between the hamlets of Holdworth and Loxley. These areas can be regarded as the local equivalent of a royal forest, reflecting the wealth and status of the lords. Unlike the Sheffield Deer Park, that covered about 2500 acres of Park Hill to the east of the city, they were not fenced but stocked with red, as opposed to fallow, deer and wardened by manorial officers called foresters who maintained a patchwork of woodlands and open areas called 'launds' where the deer would graze. As well as red and roe deer, wild boar, hares and possibly otters would be hunted and birds such as 'moorcock', red and black grouse, and plovers would be trapped or brought down with falcons. The foresters were also responsible for keeping accounts of dues from the local farmers who rented pasturage within the chase.

We know the name of one of the valley's medieval foresters because there exists in Sheffield Archives the record of court cases brought on December 22nd 1440 at Sheffield Court by one Roger Tyler, who is described as 'the Forrester of Hallfield', responsible to the Lord of the Manor for the 'maintenance of Rivelin Forest and the plentiful supply of game and boar therein', against William Drake for destroying young trees and Thomas de Shawe for driving swine from pannage (pasturage for pigs) of Hallfield. There are also cases brought against others by this forester for 'fishing without consent' and 'taking away dry wood', so he was obviously kept busy. It appears that he may have occupied a messuage or house space at the site where Hallfield House, which today sits above Dale Dyke reservoir, was later built.

The carved images of prey animals in the roof bosses and windows of Bradfield Church dating from the 1480s suggest that the Talbot lords of the manor maintained their interest in hunting over the ancient chase during the fifteenth and sixteenth centuries. By the early seventeenth century, however, the last of the Talbots had died and the Manor of Hallamshire came into the hands of the Howard family, the Dukes of Norfolk, who were largely absentees, and the whole regime of landscape maintenance within the valley changed. The deer were withdrawn from the chases and the valley's hillsides were given over entirely to the tenants of the scattered farmsteads for the grazing of their sheep and cattle. By the end of the eighteenth century the remaining commons and 'wastes' around the valley's villages of Stannington and Dungworth were enclosed by the stone walls that today divide the hillsides into neat rectangular blocks and only the names of the chase and the frith survived to tell their tale. It was only later that the lords and the newly-wealthy industrialists grasped the sporting opportunities offered by the vast tracts of moorland that stretched westwards from the upper valley.

3

A Living from the Land

A bleak, high and mountainous tract of country forms the Chapelry of Bradfield. In many parts the surface of the ground is covered with huge stones which bid defiance to all efforts of cultivation. The soil is thin and poor. The inhabitants are as rugged as their soil.

JOSEPH HUNTER, 1819

Generation after generation of valley folk have lived off this land. Although no direct evidence of prehistoric settlement as yet been discovered within the valley itself we can infer that people were here in the Bronze Age, some 3000 years ago, as a stone circle and a cluster of barrows survive on Broomhead Moor only just to the north. Evidence of even earlier visitors from over 5000 years ago are regularly picked up by walkers where the moorland peat has been eroded; tiny sharp pieces of worked flint that dropped from barbed spears of Mesolithic hunters that roamed these uplands whilst they were still wooded, hunting deer.

Back to the Romans

In April 1761 an important discovery was made by farmer Edward Nichols on a piece of common land called 'The Lawns' on the Stannington side of the Rivelin, just over the south side of the Loxley Valley. It's an ancient artefact that appears to indicate that discharged Roman soldiers were granted land and settlement rights in the area. Whilst grubbing up a large ground-fast rock he noticed two thin plates of copper or bronze, 6 inches by 5 inches beneath it. These 'plates of copper' were the celebrated Roman Military Diploma, one of only a small handful that have ever been found. One of the plates has been mysteriously lost, the other is now in the British Museum. At the time of its discovery, the Society of Antiquaries agreed that it was *"the most curious thing of the kind which had ever been discovered in England"* and that's quite some claim! Whether that is true or not this artefact has fascinated antiquarians and historians ever since, and recently a friend of mine from the valley, Mike Dyson, has written a book on the subject.

These diplomas follow a similar pattern. They were certificates of discharge, conferring Roman citizenship, with all its attendant rights and advantages, to Roman Auxiliary soldiers who had served 25 years in the Roman army; and in this case to the son of Albanus, a trooper in the 1st Cohort of Sunuci, who were originally from Belgium, and his descendants. Unfortunately his actual name has been worn away but the part of the inscription that survives reads;

To............ son of Albanus of the Sunuci, ex infantryman of cohors Sunucorum commanded by Marcus Iunius Claudianus.

The Emperor Caesar Augustus, has granted to the cavalrymen and infantrymen who served in six alae and twenty-one cohorts ....which are in Britain under Platorius Nepos, who have served twenty-five or more years and have been honourably discharged, whose names are written below, citizenship for themselves, their children and descendants, and the right of legal marriage with the wives they had when citizenship was granted to them, or, if any were unmarried, with those they later marry, but only a single one each. (A.D. 124).

The fact that this object, which must have been extremely precious to the holder himself, had been stashed here beneath a heavy rock implies that he settled here. So who was he and why was he choosing to settle here? We can only speculate. We know that the two local Roman forts, at Templebrough in the Don Valley to the east and at Brough in the Hope Valley to the west, were linked by a road that ran along the top of the opposite side of Rivelin Valley and over Stanage Edge, so our man may have tramped over the moors between the forts many times. It is recorded that Navio, the fort at Brough, was occupied for some time by the 1st Cohort of Aquitanians, a French legion, and Templebrough by the Fourth Cohort of Gauls. We know that the 1st Cohort of Sunuci, to which our soldier belonged, had been serving in Britain but not where, so this scrap of metal is the only link we have to this foreign soldier who served in the Roman army for twenty-five years before settling here, possibly farming the land and building a farmhouse for his family. And if we know about one Roman settler there must have been others of whom we have no knowledge. Maybe old established valley families have Roman ancestry.

October 20th 2019, Ughill

Although it's the first clear bright day of this whole month the low sunlight bears little warmth, one of those mornings that the hearty would term 'bracing'. Even so, it's a relief to be out under a blue sky after the greyness of the last weeks. There's water everywhere. It streams from the sodden hillside fields, swilling across the road towards the slaty grey waters of Damflask reservoir in the valley below, which, like all the valley's reservoirs, is full to overflowing. The usually calmly tinkling Ughill Brook can be heard from a couple of hundred yards away as its peaty brown water rebounds from one rounded gritstone boulder to another in foamy white cascades. There's a keen wind from the north that already gusts a few early parties of redwings straight from Siberia. The autumn is now well advanced and, if the old saying that a heavy crop of berries is likely to predict a fierce winter, we had better prepare for a stinker. The wayside hawthorns and hollies are festooned with garlands of crimson and scarlet not yet stripped by noisy flocks of wintering thrushes, blackbirds and, hopefully, waxwings that will soon be winging in from the north and east. Amongst the brown grasses and vegetation on the roadside lies something that looks very much like a wet mop head that has been used to clean a particularly filthy floor. On closer inspection it's a dead badger. It may well have been hit by a car but it's worrying that a number of such casualties have been reported in the valley recently.

A sudden metallic 'thwack' followed by a series of random retorts from the moorland on the hillside above alerts us to the presence of a shooting party. What could they be shooting? Surely all the noise of continuous gunfire would have long since scared any prey. But no, it's not grouse or pheasants that are the targeted this Sunday morning. Members of the Peak District Clay Pigeon Shooting club are meeting at Loadbrook over the hill. Clay pigeons must present a more than usually challenging target in this strong wind! I continue along Sidling Hollow, over the brook and up Tinker Bottom towards an attractive grouping of buildings clustered on the hillside amongst the trees; the hamlet of Ughill. There can't be more than a handful of homes and farm buildings but people have dwelled in this little place for more than a thousand years. Surrounding the settlement is an open landscape of rectangular green fields dotted with sheep.

"The English landscape itself, to those who know how to read it aright, is the richest historical record we possess. There are discoveries to be made in it for which no written documents exist," wrote W.G. Hoskins in 1955 in his *The Making of the English Landscape*. It is these words that come to mind as I stand, taking in this wide landscape of ancient fields and farms, stone-built barns and the apparently randomly arranged buildings of Ughill, for it was over the course of the few centuries following the withdrawal of the Romans that settlers began to move into the valley and the pattern of scattered rural settlements that we see today was gradually etched into the landscape, demonstrating the truth of Hoskin's contention that the basic elements of landscapes such as the one I'm looking at had been largely completed by the eve of the Black Death in the mid-fourteenth century. Written records of the earliest settlements are generally lacking. Only two are mentioned by name in the Domesday Book of 1086; Holdworth, on the northern valleyside, and Ughill, here on the slope above Ughill Brook. Even today these tiny hamlets are little altered, each comprising just a small handful of farm buildings. Darkness shrouds the process by which these places were founded; only their names bear witness to their origins. Holdworth was recorded as 'Haldewrth' in the Pipe Rolls of the year 1276, and as 'Haldewrde' in the Domesday Book of 1086. Both share the same meaning and derivation, which is 'Halda's settlement', derived from the pre-seventh century personal name 'Halda', from the word heald, meaning bent in the sense of a crooked back, with '-worth', a settlement or farm. Ughill is thought to have been founded in the tenth century by a group of Norwegian Vikings, with the name deriving from the Old Norse language as 'Uhgil' meaning 'Uha's Valley' or 'Uggagil' meaning 'Uggi's Valley'. In the Old Norse language, 'gill', a term more usual in the Lake District, is a steep-sided valley. So, we can assume that just prior to the Norman conquest Ughill and Holdworth had developed into Anglo-Saxon farm holdings. They were listed under the lordship of 'Healfdene' or 'Aldene' who was Lord of approximately fifty settlements, mainly across Yorkshire, Lincolnshire and Suffolk. The entry in the Domesday Book, however, tells us that the land of the manor was 'waste', possibly destroyed by William following the ravages by fire and sword inflicted in the north by his soldiers.

It is clear from some of other local place names, Dungworth, Hawksworth and Storrs, for example, that besides the two settlements that were named in the Domesday Book others must have been in existence at this time. The name of the hamlet of Storrs is a derivation of the Old Norse word 'Storth' which means a wooded place and is commonly found in the names of Viking settlements set up in woodland clearings. We don't read about the hamlet, however, until 1288 when it appears in a tenancy agreement of a local farm between the Lord, Thomas de Furnival, and Ralph del Shagh. The word 'shaw' refers to a strip of woodland. The Shaw family were to continue at the same farm for the next four centuries. The Shaws still farm at nearby Holdworth and Angie Shaw sings in our little choir in Dungworth.

Adjoining each of these ancient settlements was the 'town field' laid out in long strips in which the villagers would grow oats. These strip fields were enclosed centuries later, probably in Tudor times, and their long, narrow outlines can still be traced around Dungworth, Stannington and Ughill, standing in contrast to the large, starkly rectangular fields that were laid out following the later enclosures. The lanes around these ancient sites are narrow and twisty with quaint old names like Sidling Hollow, Trouble Wood Lane, Cow Gap Lane and Tinker Bottom, whilst long, straight roads are a heritage of the nineteenth century enclosures. Beyond the fields of these early islands of settlement the land was barren heath and moorland, increasingly grazed by sheep throughout the middle ages.

One or two early documents have emerged from the archives that throw a little light on the process by which the valley's resources were managed during these days of the early middle ages. The most celebrated of these is a charter of 1270 by which the Lord of the Manor of Hallamshire, Thomas de Furnival, granted to his tenants certain rights and privileges and confirmed existing ones. One paragraph refers to the tenants of Bradfield Dale:

> To Ellys of Ugghill and all men of Ughill, Nether Bradfield, Thornseat and Hawksworth, the herbiage, as it lies between Ugghillbrook, Eventrewick and the way leading from Hope to Sheffield, Bradrake, Seven Stones of Hardron, Weanstone to the waters of Agden for the depasturising and agisting of their own proper cattle, to be taken yearly, as they have farmed at will of my ancestors, rendering to me and my heirs four marks in silver at two terms of the year, one half at Penticost and the other at the feast of St. Martin.

Despite the antiquated language I think that the meaning is clear, that Thomas is in effect renting out the rights to local farmers to graze their cattle within Hawksworth Chase at the head of the valley. I don't know what 'four marks of silver' was worth but it seems clear that the lords were to profit by the transaction. In addition other documents indicate that the De Furnivals ran their own cattle rearing establishment known as 'Bradfield Booth', similar to various monastic bodies that held large areas of the Derwent and Edale valleys as vaccaries.

Between the twelfth and early fourteenth centuries, the population of the country increased markedly and tenant farmers gradually cleared new areas from the edges of the moors for cultivation, in which they would grow oats and rear a few livestock in small, irregularly-shaped fields. It wasn't easy ground to cultivate. These newly gained areas of ground were termed 'assarts' or later 'intakes' and are often referred to in deeds as 'mattock land' reflecting the toil required to cultivate them. By the end of the thirteenth century the pattern of small, widely-spaced farm holdings that we see today had been pretty much established. Most farms were small, ten to twenty acres being typical, but the farming families could survive by taking advantage of the grazing rights on the commons and moorlands. Many of the old farms are still organised in the same way. Hall Broom Farm near Dungworth, for example, is a sheep farm of only twenty acres but eighty acres of the adjoining moorland above is rented as grazing land.

David Hey, the indefatigable researcher into family names and derivations, has scoured medieval deeds and entries in lists of taxes to discover the story of the families that took up these rights, and has shown that many of them took their family names from the places that they lived. In 1284, for example, Adam Hawksworth, a farmer who took his surname from the place where he lived at the head of the valley, took in an eighth of an acre of new land to add to his belongings. The Hawksworths still farm in the valley and, as we have seen, the Dungworths still live locally. Other families acquired their names from landscape features, Shaw, meaning wood for example, though some were unfortunate enough to be named from some personal physical feature. A deed of 1393 tells us that a farmer with the extraordinary name of John Smallbeehind acquired eleven and a half acres of land in Holdworth, which he built up to a farm holding that was to remain in the family until the middle of the sixteenth century. Subsequent generations of the family sensibly adapted their name to Smallbend!

It may not be chance that for much of the latter half of the apocalyptic fourteenth century, when families fell prey to the scourge of the Black Death of the mid-1300s as catastrophic weather events and the plague years of 1348–50 resulted in the death of a third of the national population, none of the Sheffield Manorial Records survive, so we don't have a clear picture of how things were in our area. What is clear, however, is that by the early fifteenth century many of the names of our former farming families had disappeared from the record. It wasn't until mid-Tudor times that the population revived to the level that it was at when the Domesday Book was written. By then many of the valley families referred to in early records had died out. The only record of the Bradfields is William Bradfield, recorded farming in Bradfield in 1345, the last of the Ughills, Adam de Ughill, Roger and John, are recorded in a deed of 1295, and the Holdeworths appear in records only until 1326. It is quite possible that the Loxleys, however, held on until 1440, when Richard de Loxley was the Reeve of the Soke of Bradfield, and the Smallfields are recorded until 1672.

A small, select handful of families were to survive these upheavals and acquire extra land, bringing back into cultivation land that had fallen out of use, and during succeeding centuries one or two were able to elevate themselves to a position of the minor gentry, building the fine imposing farm buildings and halls that are a feature of the upper valley. Prominent amongst these were the Hawksworths and Greaves of Hallfield, the Moorwoods of Dungworth and the Worralls and Marriots of Ughill.

The Greaves of Hallfield

Nestling in a gentle fold overlooking Dale Dyke reservoir, surrounded by stately mature trees, stands the most distinctive and beautiful house in the upper dale, Hallfield House.

The history of this remarkable building encompasses the story of the upper dale since the Middle Ages. The present four storey house, with its distinctive double gables facing out over the waters of Dale Dyke reservoir, dates from the mid-1600s but the first we hear of Hallfield comes in a deed from 1280 indicting that there was probably already a building on this site. It is well worth reproducing this remarkable document in which Thomas de Furnival, granted to the son of John de Whyteles, land at the head of Bradfield Dale for-

> ...the depasturing and agisting of their own cattle, his heirs
> and assigns, excepting religious and Jews, of a messuage with
> appertenances, called Hallefelde in Thornsette in the soke of
> Bradfield, to hold of the grantor and his heirs freely, peacefully and
> hereditorily, with all liberties and easements and rights of pasture in
> Hawksworthe for his own beasts and their food ... paying yearly to
> the grantor and his heirs 3s 6d at the Assumption and Martinmas.

'Agistment', mentioned here, referred to pasturage in the Lord's forests and a 'messuage' is the Norman French word meaning a plot of land as the site for a house. The specific exclusion of Jews to inherit the property is particularly interesting as it comes at a time when Edward I was showing increasing antisemitism, eventually culminating in his cruel expulsion of all Jews from the country in 1290. Thomas de Furnival was evidently making sure that he was in favour with the king. The next specific reference to Hallfield is in 1318 when Adam Heggar de Romesker conveyed this piece of land, called 'Hallefelde in Thornsett', to Adam Hawksworth. Then, in 1439 Agnes de Greve surrendered a farm at Hawksworth to John Greaves Junior, and in 1565 we discover that Ralph Greaves lived at Hallfield farming forty acres of meadow and pasture, with common rights on the surrounding moorland. His family evidently prospered, continuing to farm the Hallfield land, and by the 1630s John Greaves was wealthy enough to employ a school master to instruct his seven children and was described on his death as 'Gentleman'.

By the mid part of the seventeenth century the house had been greatly altered and was much the same as we see it today, including the adjoining four bay cruck barn. In 1708 the property passed from the Greaves and was sold to the Marquis of Rockingham, Sir Thomas Wentworth of Wentworth Woodhouse, Earl Fitzwilliam, in whose family possession it continued for next 250 years. In later years it was only occasionally visited by the family for hunting parties. They did, however, continue to manage the land, planting the extensive coniferous plantations above the house along Mortimer Road that still form part of the Wentworth estates.

By 1974 the house had no longer been required by the Wentworths and was occupied only by the estate gamekeeper and prior to that by a local tenant farmer. It had been allowed to become quite derelict and in a poor state of repair and was offered for sale. The sales brochure stated:

> In need of restoration and modernisation is this most delightful Elizabethan Farm House occupying a superb situation with beautiful views to the South, over Dale Dyke and along the Loxley Valley with the open moorlands stretching to the distant horizon. The accommodation includes: a hall, 3 reception rooms, 2 kitchens, up to 12 bedrooms, a bathroom and a utility room. Outside is a series of outbuildings including stables, barns, stores and a magnificent example of a cruck barn.

And the price? This magnificent historic building was on sale for 'offers around £25,000'! In 1977 rebuilding work and restoration was carried out and Hallfield was acquired by Sir Hugh Sykes, the Sheffield businessman, who subsequently sold it to the Duckenfield family in 2007. The cruck barn, with its huge pairs of oak cruck blades, has been restored and now houses a swimming pool!

The Moorwoods of The Oaks

Like other local families the Moorwoods took their name from where they settled in the thirteenth century, a hamlet on the ridge just above Stannington where a farm and the lane that leads to it still bear their name. As with other valley families there are various deeds in the archives that detail property transfers and dealings throughout the thirteenth and fourteenth centuries by which time their fortunes were on the rise. In 1379 John de Morewod paid a shilling lay subsidy tax, one of the highest rates in the chapelry of Bradfield. He was titled 'Marshal', a term for a man who tended horses, a combination of farrier and an early vet. Coincidentally Moorwood Farm is today the Moorwood Equine Livery and Riding Centre! One William de Morwood was described in 1383 and 1406 as 'of Westmondhalgh' and in 1416 as 'of Fayrhurst'. He held land in the Ewden valley to the north in Dwarriden and Wigtwizzle and in 1411 a John de Moorwood held land in Holdworth Bank. By the time of Henry VII the family were living at The Oaks, a hall overlooking the little hamlet of Damflask.

This all indicates a local farming family on the rise, gradually acquiring wealth and status through trade and property but it's pretty dry stuff and, as with all the other local farming families, it tells us little about the people themselves. The Moorwoods however, have the distinction of being the only valley family to be commemorated in Bradfield Church with a memorial brass plaque. The well-polished shiny plate fixed to the church wall, which somehow escaped my notice on previous visits, commemorates John Morewood, who died in November 1647, and his wife, Grace, who died in the previous July. The pair are beautifully depicted, wearing Puritan dress but with elaborate ruffs, long gowns and headwear, kneeling towards one another across a draped desk on which two prayer books stand. Grace has her hands clasped in prayer whilst John appears to be clutching a large pouch of money. Between them is a depiction of their coat of arms bearing oak trees, clearly all meant to show that this is a family of some standing. What I find so fascinating about this memorial, however, is the fact that it records, and illustrates, their seven daughters, kneeling behind Grace, and nine sons lined up behind their father!

One of these sons Rowland, became a Justice of the Peace, and married Mary Gill, coincidentally of a house called 'The Oaks in Norton', Sheffield, and their son, John, inherited the house in 1681 before selling it to his bother in law Henry Gill, who subsequently built the present fine house that still stands at Norton. Another son, Andrew, married a daughter of William Spencer, the distinguished ironfounder of Attercliffe, and built The Hallows, a gabled hall that is now a golf club in Dronfield, whilst yet another son was killed in Barbados! During the eighteenth century the family, under Rowland Morewood, who in 1707 became High Sheriff of Derbyshire, continued to prosper before dying out at the end of the century. The Oaks' their house in the valley had been sold and was subsequently rebuilt as the farmhouse that still stands overlooking Damflask.

The Marriots and Ughill Hall

The Marriots, the family with a long association with Ughill Hall, were one of those old local families that had survived the upheavals of the Middle Ages. They were living in the Bradfield area in the late 1300s and in 1442 we find them living at Ughill, when John Marriot took the farm from John Dungworth. In the second half of the seventeenth century they were filemakers but gradually they were rising in status from the ranks of ordinary farmers to minor gentry. There is a legend, unsupported as far as I know by any documentary evidence, that Oliver Cromwell once visited the hall at this time. Thomas Marriot became a church Burgess in 1672, a position of standing for a filesmith, and his son, also Thomas, inherited the house at Ughill and styled himself 'Mr Marriot of Ughill Hall'. The present building, which can only be glimpsed through the hedge, dates from his rebuilding in 1697. In 1712 he was of sufficient standing to found a school at Bradfield and endow it with ten pounds a year. The family were leading Dissenters and Thomas was able to bequeath Spout House Farm for the use of a dissenting minister at Underbank Chapel. By the time that Benjamin, his son, died without male heir, the family had been at Ughill for over 300 years.

In the early twentieth century, the hall was owned by Sheffield solicitor Charles Edward Vickers of The Manor House, Ecclesall, who used it as a summer shooting lodge. In Bradfield church there is a brass plaque with the following inscription:

TO THE GLORY OF GOD AND IN PROUD AND LOVING MEMORY OF
CHARLES GOLDTHORP VICKERS, CAPTAIN 2/4
(HALLAMSHIRE) BATTALION

YORK & LANCASTRE REGIMENT, 62ND DIVISION.
FELL IN ACTION AT BOURLON WOOD FRANCE.
NOVEMBER 22ND 1917 AGED 27,
AND WAS BURIED IN GRAINCOURT CEMETERY.
YOUNGEST SON OF MR & MRS C.E. VICKERS, UGHILL HALL, BRADFIELD.

Sadly I can discover nothing of his life except that he was a renowned bowler at cricket. However, in an utterly bizarre twist of fate this would not be the last time that 'France' and 'death' became linked to the story of Ughill Hall.

When I began writing this account of my wanderings in the Loxley Valley and the curious events and tales that I would discover I hadn't anticipated the extraordinary amount of death that I would encounter. I suppose that I shouldn't have been surprised since all history to some extent is about dead people but the unusual circumstances in which so many people in the valley have died at one time or another strikes me as distinctly strange. There are deaths in industrial accidents and diseases, a more than usual count of suicides and a massive toll of drownings. There have also been, tragically, some quite celebrated murders. The earliest, when Robin of Loxley supposedly murdered his father, leading to his life as an outlaw is probably mythical but the murder of Nathen Andrews by Frank Fearn on Loxley Common was certainly true and we'll come back to the gruesome tale later. The terrible murders that occurred here at Ughill Hall, however, were well within living memory.

The Ughill murders

In April 1986 a man called Ian Wood, a solicitor and the ex-secretary of the Law Society in Sheffield, took the rental of Ughill Hall, and moved in with his mistress Danielle Ledez, having left his wife Margaret and his three children. Two years earlier his father, a director of a Sheffield steel company, had shot himself with a revolver. After the inquest the gun was handed to his son who had bought fifty rounds of ammunition in Sheffield for the .38 Enfield revolver.

Danielle Ledez was a French teacher from Amiens, France, who moved to Ughill Hall with Wood and her two children, Stephanie aged three and Christopher aged five. She was in the process of divorcing their father, her second husband, Colin Lloyd, a teacher from Sheffield. At approximately 12 midnight on 21 September 1986, Wood went to the playroom in the mansion and killed his mistress Danielle Ledez by shooting her once in the head. She was ten weeks pregnant by Wood. In a statement Wood later told the police what happened next.

> The children were downstairs... I used a cushion to stop the noise and shot her... I went downstairs for Stephanie. I took her up to the bedroom to play 'hidey-ho.' I covered her head and shot her twice. At first she was looking straight at me. Her eyes were open. I had to be sure she was dead, so I closed my eyes and shot her again. Then I went down to Christopher who was eating a tomato salad. I told him I had a surprise for him and to close his eyes and not to peep. I told him to lie down on the floor and I put a towel over his head and shot twice. I went down to the kitchen and then went upstairs to pack. As I went past the bathroom I heard a low moan. He was not dead. I picked up a thick pole and hit him four or five times until the stick broke.

Wood changed clothes, packed his bags, and left the house shortly afterwards, leaving the weapon, the .38 Enfield revolver, in the kitchen with one live round left. The police went to the mansion the following evening after receiving a telephone call from Wood. Finding all the doors and windows locked, they broke down the door. Christopher was rushed to Sheffield Children's Hospital with severe head injuries and was placed on life support. By a miracle of some sort, Christopher was to survive. Following the discovery of the bodies, the police appealed to Wood to turn himself in and warned members of the public not to approach him as he may be armed. Wood's wife Margaret and their three children were put under police protection immediately, as was Ledez's husband Colin Lloyd.

Two days later Wood made a series of telephone calls to Brenda Tunney, a reporter for the local newspaper *Sheffield Weekly Gazette*. Wood refused to disclose his location but claimed the purpose of the calls was to 'put his side'. By 26 September he had made at least eight phone calls. On 27 September, Wood called Tunney four times asking about funeral arrangements for Ledez and her daughter and the following day made three more calls to Tunney and threatened suicide, claiming he killed because of love and desperation, not anger and hate.

It was later established that Wood had gone to a pub after committing the killings and then, over the course of the next few days, travelled to Dover where he caught a ferry to France. On 29 September he joined a public tour of Amiens Cathedral, which stood near Ledez's birthplace, but, when on the roof, he broke away from the tour group, climbed over the parapet, and clung to a gargoyle about 200 feet above the ground, threatening to commit suicide by jumping off. He had left a note with a member of staff at the cathedral shortly beforehand informing them of his intention to commit suicide, which had prompted them to call the police, and had also telephoned Ledez's family to inform them of his intention to commit suicide.

A crowd of several hundred people gathered to watch from below. The police, firemen, the church's priest, and members from the British Consulate pleaded with Wood for seven hours, at which point Wood surrendered. Wood later claimed that he did not wish his family to see his fall on television, describing the scene as a circus. He was flown back to the UK on 19 November where he was remanded in custody.

On 1 December 1986, the prosecution charged Wood on two counts of murder and one count of attempted murder, for Danielle, Stephanie, and Christopher, respectively. He also faced a charge of stealing £84,000 from clients he represented in property deals. He pleaded not guilty to the murder of Danielle and instead entered a manslaughter plea on the grounds that they had agreed to a suicide pact. However, he pleaded guilty to the murder of Stephanie and the attempted murder of Christopher. He also pleaded guilty to stealing the £84,000 from clients. The prosecution did not accept the manslaughter plea and pursued a trial for the murder of Danielle.

At his trial at Sheffield Crown Court Wood gave a detailed account of a five-point agreement he claimed to have made with Ledez as to what to do after the killings and before his suicide which included visiting a French church to light candles for Ledez and her children, sending a detailed explanation of the deaths to the press and killing Ledez's husband, Colin Lloyd. On the final day of the trial, the prosecution argued that Wood's suicide threat on Amiens Cathedral was not genuine and was done only to disguise his true motive. Gilbert Gray, leading the defence, argued that Wood had nothing to gain from lying about a suicide pact because he would be sentenced to life imprisonment for the murder and attempted murder of Ledez's children anyway but the jury unanimously rejected Wood's claim that he killed Ledez as part of a suicide pact and found him guilty of murder. Justice Taylor sentenced Wood to life imprisonment for each murder, twelve years for the attempted murder, and three years for the specimen charges of theft from clients. Wood was struck off the Law Society register and the Law Society Compensation Fund paid out at least £240,000 in compensation to the theft victims.

Memorial to a Drowned Girl

Before leaving Ughill I turn right over the brow of the hill and find myself looking down over the wide expanse of the upper valley towards Dale Dyke. Standing beside the road here is the most curious monument in the valley, a stone-built structure with a gable end that extends upwards into a triangular twelve-foot-high spire, built into the roadside wall. It is said that the monument records yet another local drowning tragedy, having been built to cover a large water trough in which a little girl drowned in 1832. Whilst this story has been often repeated I can find no further details. Who was she? Is the story true? Who organised the erection of such an elaborate memorial? We just don't know.

What we do know, however, and what makes the monument even stranger, is that the inscription across the front has been clumsily hacked away. Only the word 'Bradfield' and a date in Roman numerals can still just about be picked out. The story behind this is curious in itself. Edgefield Farm, on whose land this strange monument stands, belonged to the local Drabble family. The Drabbles had moved to Edgefield in about 1926, having built up a successful business operating a gannister and clay mine and processing plant at Ughill, and restyled the farm as 'Edgefield Hall'. Following the death of his father and brother, William Drabble, known as Billy, took charge of the business and it is believed that it was Billy Drabble, well known for his somewhat eccentric behaviour, who erased the date and name from the water monument during the last war to cause confusion to the Germans should they ever land at Bradfield! This would appear to be comical but there could be a rather sad reason for Billy's behaviour. During the First World War he had served as a private in the Coldstream Guards and had been deeply affected by his experiences.

Farmsteads and their Cruck Barns

Here at Ughil, on the opposite side of the road to the hall, stands the grade II listed buildings of Ughill Manor, an early eighteenth century farmhouse, though not actually a manor house. As I pass the gate a large dog leaps from its kennel in the yard, barking loudly and I'm relieved to see that it's restrained by a long chain. The so-called manor is an attractive long building that incorporates farmhouse, barn and stabling that has clearly undergone considerable alteration, with new windows and a blue slate roof. Across the yard from the house, however, stands a huge ancient looking barn set at an angle, its mossy stone-slabbed roof stretching almost to the ground. I'm pleased to be invited by the owner to look inside. This is an important, early timber-framed building, erected in early Tudor times. In fact its timbers have been dated to 1504, which makes it one of the earliest buildings in whole Sheffield region. On entering through the huge pair of threshing doors I see four colossal A-shaped frames of oak spanning the space, stretching from the ground at the base of the stone walls to the roof apex, where they are pinned together with wooden pegs. It's clear that it's these roughly-shaped timbers that support the roof span, not the walls. The immediate impression is of the strength of the massive timbers and their age.

Even though good building stone was readily available, before the sixteenth century all the valley's buildings would have been constructed like this, from wood. There were two basic systems of building timber framed structures. The first, known as 'post-and-truss,' is the more familiar. It entails building a box-like structure from four vertical posts and connecting them with horizontal beams. The 'black-and-white' buildings, such as Sheffield's Bishop's House, are of this type. In our region, however, along the eastern slopes and valleys of the Pennines, a different and more unusual tradition prevailed which is known as 'cruck' building, in which the roof was supported by a series of 'A' frames, known as 'pairs of crucks,' each fastened with tie beams and connected together with a massive ridge beam.

This method of construction involved finding a suitable tree, usually an oak, with a curved trunk or large main branch. This was then squared and cut in half lengthwise to produce two matching 'cruck-blades' which were then erected to form an A-frame with the main tie-beam joining the two blades and projecting out to the level of the eaves. The advantage of this system was that the roof was wholly supported by the crucks, and, since the walls are not load-bearing, they could be constructed of any available material and easily be changed when need arose. Thus cruck-frame buildings which were originally timber-clad have generally been cased in stone or brick and the evidence of the construction method is often hidden. The space between each pair of crucks is called a 'bay', so a barn constructed of four pairs of crucks would have three bays and each bay would have had a different use. In the earliest times the family would live in one bay, the animals in another and the last used for food storage. The vast majority of the 120 or so cruck-built buildings that survive in south-west Yorkshire are barns, and the Loxley valley preserves a unique concentration of these listed historical structures.

There is no general agreement as to where or when cruck-frame construction originated. Experts disagree as to whether it is indigenous or came from the Continent. Local tradition in our region used to assert that it belonged to a Celtic tradition and that surviving cruck buildings are Anglo-Saxon in origin. This is understandable since they conjure up images of Saxon or Viking mead halls but such conjecture has been refuted by scientific analysis based on dendrochronology (tree ring) dating. The earliest examples turn out to be Medieval with the tradition continuing just into the eighteenth century. Of the ones in the valley which have been dendro dated, the earliest is the barn at Hall Broom farm, Dungworth, dated 1495/6. Ughill Manor Barn was built in 1504, Hallfield House barn about a year later and Well House Farm, Stannington, between 1591 and 1600, so the evidence suggests that there was a span of a little over the hundred years of the sixteenth century in which these surviving barns were built. In other words they can broadly be regarded as Tudor buildings, surviving evidence of the growing national prosperity in Elizabethan England that resulted from the surge in trade and industry.

On the walk back to Dungworth I call at Hall Broom Farm hoping to have a look at another cruck barn, the earliest cruck barn in the valley. The owner, farmer Andrew Bramhall, is only too pleased to show me this most remarkable building. It stands across the top of the farmyard, a long low building with a massive blue slate roof in some need of repair. To the left the threshing doors stand open, the similar opening on the opposite side having been walled up. A single storey cowhouse, now used for chickens, extends from the front, its front wall supported by four huge rough gritstone posts. At one end of the barn stone steps lead from the yard to a second floor where, according to the owner, the family would have slept, above the stable for warmth. Inside the barn the four curved pairs of oak crucks, standing on heavy stone supports called 'stylobates', soar to the apex of the roof, smothered in ancient dusty cobwebs. It's a monumental building. There is no ridge beam, the roof is supported by the horizontal purlins and the structure is made rigid by 'wind braces' which form triangles between the crucks and the purlins. The main 'tie beam' between the central pair of cruck blades is missing. A rough stone wall has been built to wall off the lowest bay, which is divided by a floor reached from the stone steps outside. Hall Broom is now a sheep farm and animals are sometimes sheltered in the barn in winter so it is probable that this building has been in constant use since 1495!

In virtually every location in the valley the barn predates the existing farmhouse. The suggestion that part of the barn at Hall Broom may have provided the accommodation for the family therefore raises a question as to whether this was generally the case. In fact, as far as I know, only a couple of timber-framed farmhouses still stand in the valley, at Fair Flatts Farm, Holdworth and Pond Farmhouse, Stannington, though others may exist, having been encased in later stone walling. These two may well help to answer my question.

Pond Farmhouse stands amongst a group of stone-built cottages and buildings that were originally part of a farm on the opposite side of the road to the row of shops in the centre of Stannington. The interior retains substantial remains of a medieval three-bay, cruck-framed open-hall house. Although the actual date of its construction is unknown it has stood here for at least 400 years and therefore can lay claim to being one of the very few surviving late medieval buildings in Sheffield. A plan drawn in 1747 depicts a pond on the site of today's shops that is labelled 'Old Motte' and an adjoining building, since demolished, is labelled 'The Mannor House', so Pond Farmhouse may have been part of this group. There is nothing on the exterior of the building to suggest such an age, partly because it has undergone considerable alteration, having been clad in stone at some date and having undergone complete restoration in the 1970s to create a modern interior. It does, however, still retain its distinctive feature; the oak framework of three pairs of heavy curved cruck blades that originally supported the roof, now embedded in the walls.

Fortunately Pond Farmhouse was surveyed and plans drawn up by Stanley Jones and Peter Ryder of the South Yorkshire Archaeology Service in 1977 when the building was semi-derelict. Their conclusion was that this was, in its earliest form, a medieval hall house, of four bays with the open hall occupying the central two bays. To one end of the building was the hearth and cross-passage, with a screen to divide it off from the hall. At the other end would have been the parlour and sleeping space above. They dated the building to no later than the fifteenth century, all of which seems to closely parallel the similarly constructed barn at Hall Broom.

At Fair Flatts Farm, on the hillside above Damflask, and apparently wrongly named on the OS map as 'New Lathes Farm', is a long timber-framed building of post and truss construction rather than cruck-built, comprising a long barn and a cottage at the uphill end, like one of the long houses that are a feature of the Peak District, that housed the animals and crops at one end and the family at the other. Its timber frame is now enclosed with gritstone rubble walls and it features a huge stone-flagged roof and small windows tucked under the eaves. Its grade 2 listing marks it simply as 'probably seventeenth century'.

December 2019, Bowsen and Cliff Rocher.

It's a stiffish walk up the steep hillside from Agden to the barn that I've come to look at but, although I might be a bit out of breath, it's worth the climb through the plantation when I get up there. The view is magnificent. On a clear bright day like this the smooth cliff face of the rocky outcrop known as Cliff Rocher that overlooks Agden reservoir shines with an almost silvery sheen. It looks as though it's the result of some ancient landslip, the oak-wooded ground beneath being tumbled and disturbed. Below the eastern edge of the cliff, isolated in farmer's fields, stands a low building that settles comfortably into the hillside sheltered by old lichen-covered sycamores; a lone cruck barn, the only one in the valley on access land open to the public. It sits squarely on a small shoulder of flattish land looking out over the valley below. It has the peculiar name of 'Bowsen' which I think may have something to do with badgers. To the right-hand side of the barn the ground is disturbed, nettles grow through piles of tumbled masonry and timber. Now I understand why the barn stands alone. These are the sad ruins of Rocher Head Farm that was, like nearby Frost Farm and Agden House, one of the many of the valley's old farmsteads that were unfortunately demolished in the early 1960s and 70s by the water company to protect the water gathering grounds from contamination. It had been the home of the Saddington family. In the churchyard at High Bradfield there is a memorial seat, dated 1965, which bears the following inscription: 'In memory of Joseph and Lucy Ann Saddington also son Percy and daughter Catherine Mary of Rocher Head, Bradfield'.

It's disappointing to see that, although the barn has a Grade 2 listing, the original stone-slabbed roof has been replaced by one of corrugated iron. This dates from the time in the 1980s when it was used for educational purposes but at least this historic building has survived. Once I heave my boots out of the deep mud that surrounds the doorway I venture inside. The floor is rough, hard-packed earth, simply now being used as a sheep shelter. From the base of the stone walls rise three pairs of roughly shaped wooden crucks standing on padstones to prevent them from rot. The horizontal tie-beams are low, not even head height. Each set of curved crucks cross at the apex, fixed with wooden pegs. It's amazing to think that these timbers probably date from the late seventeenth century. Neatly stacked stone roof flags are piled beside the wall. Except for the unfortunate roof the building is wonderfully authentic and deserves sympathetic restoration. Let's hope that it may one day be fully restored.

Holly Hags

The farmsteads and barns that dot the hillsides reflect that throughout the long history of the valley the mainstay of the farmers has been the dairy herd and the flock of sheep. Farming practices, however, have changed over time. In such upland areas of the north and west of England as this it was common practice to feed livestock on holly during the winter. A diarist and collector of antiquarian facts called Abraham de la Pryme, who came from Hatfield beyond Doncaster, visited the Loxley Valley in 1696 and regarded the local custom curious enough to note in his diary the following observations:

> At and about Bradfield they feed their sheep in winter with holly leaves and bark, which they eat more greedily than any grass. To every farm there is so many holly trees and the more there is the farm is dearer but great care is taken to plant great numbers of them in all farms thereabouts. And all these holly leaves are smooth-leaved and not prickly. As soon as the sheep sees the shepherd come with an axe in his hand they follow him to the first tree he comes at and stands all in a round about the tree, expecting impatiently the branch to fall, which when fallen, all as many as can eats thereof, and the shepherd going forward to another tree, all those that could not come unto the eating of the first, follow him to this, and so on. As soon as they have eaten all the leaves they begins on the bark and pairs it all off.

This sounds a very unlikely, not to say uncomfortable, foodstuff but in fact the fresh young leaves of holly lack sharp prickles and are very nutritious, and the practice harks way back to the days when the officers of the medieval lords of the manor would feed holly leaves and branches to the deer in winter. The accounts of the forester of Bradfield in 1441 listed "for holly sold there for the fodder of animals in winter." John Harrison, in his exhaustive survey of the Manor of Hallamshire in 1637, lists "A hagg of hollin in the wood and under the Toft Ends at Stannington" that was rented by Thomas Revill and another 24 holly tenants are similarly listed. Various local names such as Hollin Dale and Hagg Hill preserve a memory of this custom. The word 'Hagg', by the way, comes from the old Norse word 'Hagi' referring to a pasture; yet another bit of evidence that the Vikings settled in the valley. By the early eighteenth century this practice was beginning to die out. In 1710 the Duke of Norfolk's bailiff reported that some of the holly hags were unlett and many destroyed. The deer had been removed from Loxley chase and the last account of holly rents was dated 1737 when a Bradfield man agreed to take "all that hag of Hollin called Ugghill Wood."

The Great Rebuilding

By the end of the seventeenth century, the local tradition of timber building was drawing to a close. Greater prosperity as a result of a thriving agricultural economy, along with a desire for privacy and comfort, brought about what has been termed 'A Great Age of Rebuilding in stone'. When the traveller Celia Fiennes journeyed through the area in 1697 she noted that *"there are many fine houses, newly built of freestone."* In fact there are an astonishing 141 grade II listed buildings in the Bradfield Ward of Sheffield, and the largest proportion of these are farmhouses, barns and agricultural outbuildings that date from precisely the era of the great rebuilding of the late seventeenth and early eighteenth centuries. Relatively few farmsteads throughout the country survive from this early date, making this collection in the valley nationally important.

The farmhouse at Hall Broom Farm at Dungworth, dates from 1620, a date that is carved on the door lintel, and its architectural features, mullion windows, drip moulds over the windows and kneelers to the stone slabbed roof proclaim its age, though this is over a hundred years more recent than the adjoining four-bay cruck barn and cowhouse. The oldest building in present-day Holdworth is Far House Farm occupied by the Shaw family. The Grade II listed farmhouse, dating from the late seventeenth century, looks out over the valley above Damflask amidst a patchwork of ancient fields and dry gritstone walls. Of a similar date is Ughill Hall where a stone on the front wall had the inscription 'Thomas Marriot, 1697'. Walker House Farm, near the Dale Dyke embankment, with its superb five bay cruck barn and adjoining cowhouse, dates from the early seventeenth century....and so the list of these important heritage buildings goes on; Broggin House at Strines, Lower Thornseat Farmhouse, Briers House Farm, Tom Hill Farm and the beautiful farmhouse and cruck barn at Smallfield Farm overlooking Agden.

But today one person's heritage is another's headache and one person's historic building may be another's millstone round the neck. Maintaining a seventeenth century farm building in good repair is an expensive proposition, especially at a time when farming marginal land like this is a precarious way to make a living. Living in a listed building imposes its own difficulties and restrictions and the fact that half of the valley falls within the Peak District National Park imposes on the owners further planning considerations and another potential layer of bureaucracy. The ownership of a timber-framed seventeenth century cruck barn brings a particular headache as they are generally unsuitable for modern farming practices. Most are simply used to store old equipment. Some, like the huge barn at Walker House Farm, have lost their original roof. Here it has been replaced by unattractive corrugated asbestos and the ancient cruck timbers are riddled with woodworm. The seventeenth century cruck barn at Woodseats Farm on Windy Bank at Low Bradfield was in a ruinous state with no roof but has now been protected by the erection of a corrugated iron roof like the Bowsen barn. Others, despite their historic value, are in a precarious state. Granting them 'listed status' might prevent their demolition but it doesn't provide the funding to prevent them from falling down. One way to preserve the structures, as has happened to the cruck barns at Throstle's Nest in Storrs, at Hallfield House and at Tom Hill Farm, Dungworth, is to convert them, with permission, to dwellings.

One heritage building in the valley that has suffered badly over the years is, however, currently being rescued. Spout House, on the edge of Stannington, which is claimed to date from 1545 with additions in 1678 (English Heritage lists it as 'probably late seventeenth century'), is one of the most architecturally interesting of the valley's historic farmsteads. An undated, thirteenth-century deed mentions Le Sputesyke as a boundary here, and another deed of 1316 records *"all that messuage, with the outbuildings, land and tenements at le Spouthous."* Its name was probably derived from a water outlet, and there still stands a most impressive series of gritstone troughs on Spout Lane, just opposite the house. Joseph Hunter in 'Hallamshire' tells us that it was the home to many generations of the Morton family, whose coat of arms over the door featured three black ravens.

Until 1965, when it was sold, it was worked as a traditional family dairy farm. Tragically, it was badly damaged in a fire in 2016 in which the occupants, Leonard and Freda Ewing, who were both in their 90s, and were said to be somewhat reclusive, died. This was not the first tragedy to strike the farm for it is said that a previous owner cut his throat in the cowshed but as this was not successful he then hung himself in the dairy. Following the fire which gutted the historic building it stood empty until listed for auction with a guide price of £475,000, *"to suit a buyer looking for a large-scale refurbishment project."* Remarkably a buyer came forward and today the gutted ruins of Spout House are enveloped in scaffolding and undergoing very welcome restoration.

The Decline of the Woodlands

As well as the changes in farming practices and building methods that took place during the late seventeenth and early eighteenth centuries the wooded landscape itself became rapidly denuded of trees. In Sir Walter Scott's novel *Ivanhoe*, written in 1819, the opening lines hark back to a local forested landscape that had long since disappeared;

In that pleasant part of merry England which is watered by the
River Don there extended in ancient times, a large forest covering
the greater part of the beautiful hills and valleys which lie between
Sheffield and the pleasant town of Doncaster. The remains of this
ancient woodland, remain to be seen at the noble seats of Wentworth
and Wharncliffe and around Rotherham.

As early as 1637 John Harrison had noted that *"Hallamshire was ideal for
the placement of ironworks on account of its great store of stately timber"* and local
South Yorkshire ironmaster Lionel Copley soon had his eye on the Loxley
Valley woodlands. In his Notes written in 1741 John Wilson of Broomhead
Hall laments that the hollies had been grubbed up, the oaks felled and that
few trees were left. He reports a scene of general desolation that *"has much
injured the appearance of the hillsides."* The devastation caused to the landscape
by Copley's destruction of the woodlands was even immortalised in a formerly
well-known doggerel verse that sums up the depth of local feeling against it:

If Mr Copley had never been born
Or in his cradle died,
Loxley Chase had never been torn,
Nor many a brave wood beside.

Lionel Copley died in 1675 and the monopoly of iron production in South
Yorkshire was acquired by a syndicate of gentleman ironmasters under the
Spencers of Cannon Hall near Barnsley. Their manager, John Fell, who ran
Attercliffe Forge, obtained the lease to Stannington Wood on the opposite side
of the valley to the already treeless Chase and clear felled it to feed his furnaces
in 1728. Forge Valley Comprehensive school and its extensive playing fields
now occupy this formerly wooded site.

Just as the valley's woodlands were disappearing, its wide, open moorland was
being converted to grassland pasture in a regular pattern of starkly rectangular
fields, enclosed in straight dry-stone walls, according to plans approved by
Commissioners such as those that enacted the 'Wadsley and Loxley Chase
Parliamentary Enclosure' awarded in 1789. There were still a few bits of
common land around Storrs and the other ancient focusses of settlement
until the end of the eighteenth century but in 1787 Charles Howard, eleventh
Duke of Norfolk and other landowners proposed to enclose these areas. The

proposal predictably met with some hostility by 'several of the freeholders and inhabitants' but none of the challengers to the policy owned enough land to defy the large landowners and the valley's few remaining commons were enclosed between 1791 and 1805.

August 2020, Dungworth

I've driven the six or seven miles from home, up hill and down dale, over to Dungworth to call at my daughter's cottage to go for a walk with the grandchildren. I pause as usual, conscious of the quiet and the rural aroma of fresh air, to take in the view right down the valley towards the distant hillside overlooking central Sheffield that was once marked by the famous dry ski slopes. Rather disconcertingly a black and white cow looks down six feet above me from the top of the wall that supports the sloping field by the road.

Dungworth is a small village of some ninety houses that sits on an eastward facing shelf strung out along a couple of roads. Although it isn't mentioned by name in the Domesday Book, it must have existed as a settlement before the Norman Conquest because the name ending *'worth'* derives from the Anglo Saxon meaning a small enclosure. We can only speculate how it acquired the first part of the unfortunate name but it had been suggested that it could refer to a house built into the ground or one having a turf roof. The OS map marks, in antiquated gothic script, 'Dungworth Cross (site of)' at a spot beside the road into the valley but, as far as I know, there is no written record of a medieval cross having ever stood here! It may well refer to a lost waymarker on this old packhorse route.

It was, and to a large extent still is, essentially a farming community with ten farmsteads in the vicinity, many of which had been in the same families, the Drabbles, Greys, Hawksworths, Tricketts and Dungworths, for centuries. There's no physical focus to the village. Gradually the spaces between the gritstone farmhouses have been filled with cottages and more recent houses in an apparently random pattern. It's not quaint or picturesque in any way. The Royal, the village pub, the primary school and the Village Hall are the centre of village life but the two nonconformist nineteenth century chapels have closed due to falling membership and have been converted to private houses. In recent years many properties in the village have been purchased and modernised by young professional people who work outside the valley.

It's a pleasant day for a short walk but the girls can be persuaded to accompany us only if we bribe them with the promise of a stop at the ice cream parlour at the farmyard of Cliffe House Farm at Hill Top. On such a sunny day the field next to 'Our Cow Molly' will be packed with cars as it's become quite a popular destination for families. Our grandchildren have been such good customers that Graham Andrew, the farmer who runs the enterprise with his son Eddie, has named two of this year's calves after the twins! Our Cow Molly, as the dairy enterprise is called, sells fifty varieties of ice cream from the farmyard shop including Cora's Chaos (pink with marshmallows), jam roly-poly and my favourite, liquorice.

The business was built out of desperation. Despite having built up a successful milk delivery business, the Andrew family were in despair that the farm was losing money for every pint sold to the major dairy and they looked for a way to resolve the issue. The number of local dairy farms in Dungworth had fallen from six to two so the farm's future looked bleak. Graham's son, Eddie, investigated the idea of using the excess milk to make ice cream and the rest is history, with the brand now well-established. One particularly successful partnership has been developed with Sheffield University who, wishing to reduce emissions and minimise the negative effects of transporting goods long distance, have contracted for milk from the farm's dairy to supply all nineteen of the university cafes. This has enabled Our Cow Molly to invest in a brand new £500,000 dairy to increase the maximum weekly output from 8,000 to 40,000 litres and also led to the dairy winning the 'Future Food Award' at the BBC Farming Awards 2016. Do they have a cow called Molly? Well, not exactly. The catchy name was coined by Graham when he came up with the jingle: "Don't put it in your supermarket trolley, Buy your milk from our cow 'Molly'."

But if the Andrews family at Hill Top have found a formula by which the traditional cattle husbandry of the farm can be maintained, others have branched out in even more innovative ways. Two generations of the Gill family of Watt House Farm, high above the valley at Bradfield, have gone from milking 100 cows a day to brewing over 100,000 pints of beer a week. Bradfield Brewery completed its first brew on 26th April 2005 and this September has celebrated its 5000th. The enterprise has been incredibly successful. With its range of popular ales named after breeds of cows, the brewery has been able to maintain the link with its farming heritage. Not only can the beers be enjoyed far and wide but they have now purchased several of the ailing local pubs and are breathing life into the local economy.

On the road near Loadbrook above Dungworth, another enterprising farmer has literally branched out, having founded The Sheffield Christmas Tree Company in 2006 when he planted the first of 20,000 Christmas trees. It's now possible to pick your own tree from the selection of firs and spruces, browse the gift shop, and have a coffee in the log cabins built from shipping containers. But this doesn't exhaust the remarkable selection of enterprises that have developed here at Cow Gap Farm. Alongside the lane a large lake has been dug and stocked with fish; barbell, tench and carp, that attracts day fishermen from miles around to enjoy the fishing and the peaceful views over the valley. And in case you are having a party, the farm also houses Sheffield Bouncy Castle Hire!

Rural Cutlers

Having licked the last of our ice creams we set off down the path with the curious name of 'Pudding Poke' across the hillside fields. This is a circular walk around the village and the bottom of the path meets Dungworth Green, the narrow lane that leads to Storrs. Beside the lane stands a farmhouse called 'Syke'. Now renovated as a modern home, it's a building that has obviously undergone many alterations and additions. At least four different sections of the building, each diminishing in size, stretch down the hill.

This building is a survival of an important local way of life in which many of the local farmers combined their agricultural activities with the production of knives. *"The greater part of the inhabitants of the Lordship of Hallamshire do consist of cutlers"* was how this practice was described in the introduction to the Act that incorporated the Cutler's Company of Hallamshire in 1624. Like the Andrews at Our Cow Molly, the men who farmed the marginal Pennine slopes of Yorkshire had long been familiar with the idea of having a second string to their bow. In the West Riding to the north it was the weaving of woollen cloth that went alongside working the land or tending livestock but around Sheffield it was working with metal. Nailmakers, filesmiths, scythesmiths, scissor makers and knife makers of all kinds are to be found in the Bradfield parish registers. One record of 1437 refers to *"A messuage and an oxgang of land in Bradfield, formerly held by Robert Tynker, Naylor"* but this was already a centuries old industry, based on the availability of iron, coal, sandstone, timber and water, nurtured in the rural communities of the local valleys through skills passed down from father to son down the generations. They plied their trades in basic workshops adjoining their farms or outbuildings, pursuing a dual occupation, combining the production of edge tools with their farming activities. My daughter's long, narrow cottage in Dungworth has a date stone of 1832. One end of the building had been a cutler's forge, occupied by a knife forger called Henry Wragg.

Throughout the seventeenth and eighteenth centuries Dungworth, Wadsley and Stannington were at the centre of this local trade. In 1819 Joseph Hunter wrote that the cutlers were using the same methods and making the same articles as were their forefathers of the seventeenth century. There's a Sheffield saying that 'It on'y taks one an' thruppence te mak a cutler', and it certainly didn't take much to set up a smithy; a hearth with a pair of bellows, a large anvil, locally known as a 'stiddy', and a water trough to harden the blades, was sufficient to start. Sometimes there would be a glazing frame turned by a foot treadle for polishing the blades. A workbench would stand beneath the open window at which bone, horn or wooden handles would be riveted to the blades. Up until the late eighteenth century the cutlers would take the item right through all the processes, renting a trough at the nearby wheel turned by the river where the blades would be ground. By the nineteenth century the pocket knives that were produced here were not generally of the highest quality and were often referred to disparagingly as 'Wadsley knock-ons'.

One particular local pattern of folding knife, however, was to make a surprising impact across the Atlantic. The legendary story of this knife says that in 1667 one of the cutlers in Stannington, Obadiah Barlow, began producing the rugged-looking, single-bladed folding knife that was to bear his name. Barlow's grandson, John, emigrated to America taking the pattern with him. The patent to the Barlow name was passed down through the family and was finally purchased by the John Russell Cutlery Company of Green River, Mass. who then mass-produced their 'Barlows' by the million during the pioneering days of the nineteenth century. One commentator is quoted as saying that;-

> A real Barlow was a prized treasure for small boys, farmers and whittlers (even Huckleberry Finn). Barlow jackknives from Russell Cutlery trimmed more fishlines, cut more leather and reduced the proportions of more sticks of wood than any other knives in American history.

The group of buildings at Syke is probably the most complete survival of a rural forge that demonstrates the close association between farming and cutlery production. The farmhouse itself, which, dating from about 1870, is later than the attached buildings, stands at the top, followed by a windowless cowhouse followed by an eighteenth century smithy with its open three-light window space. A second similar window has been blocked by the addition of the stable below it. The farm itself had only nine acres of poor land, partly disturbed by coal mining, sufficient only to support a few livestock, which makes it easy to understand why the dual occupation was so essential. The Barnett family in the eighteenth and the Nichols in the nineteenth occupied the farm and the last cutler to use the forge was John Ward Nichols in the 1860s. Could this be the same premises that the cutler Richard Bacon surrendered a third share of in 1613, and which was described in the records as *"an oxgang of land at Dungworth-Storrs, along with a new barn, an outshutt called the calf-house and a worke-house and croft at the end of a dwelling house."* It certainly fits the description. Most of the cutlers were poor, simply eking out a living but a few became men of some substance. For instance the inventory of Thomas Dungworth Jnr, a cutler of Stannington in 1690, shows that his house had six well-furnished rooms and that he had two stythies (anvils) and livestock amounting to a value of £108.

November 17th 2020, Far House Farm, Holdworth

The climb straight up the hillside from Damflask to the tiny group of farmsteads that constitutes the hamlet of Holdworth demonstrates the inadequacy of maps to depict three dimensions. Although the map tells me that I'm only one kilometre from Damflask I've actually travelled further than that due to the steep gradient and it seems a world away from the valley floor up here. I stand, taking in the bird's-eye view overlooking the whole breadth of the wide valley and beyond. The wind is relentless, flattening the tall grass and ragged brown roadside weeds. The Vikings who founded the settlement must have been a hardy lot, as are Angie (one of the extensive Crapper clan) and Robert Shaw who farm here at Far House Farm with their son. Grade 2 listed Far House is typical of the solidly-built gritstone long farmhouses with a heavy, stone-slabbed roof, barns at one end and the house at the other. The tiny mullioned windows, roof kneelers and blocked barn owl hole in the rear gable wall suggest a dating from the late seventeenth or early eighteenth century.

Robert has farmed the area for at least fifty years and is typical of local farmers in having to adapt to changing market demands. Most of the local farms up to the 1960s were small dairy farms, milking only eight to sixteen cows, relying on making daily deliveries from wagons to customers in Hillsbrough or Walkley. As time went on, with milk prices guaranteed by the Milk Marketing Board, some farms expanded their herds and prospered, others failed. Robert prospered, and by 1999 he was milking ninety-nine cows daily. Supermarket price wars, however, meant that it was becoming difficult to make a living and the work involved, from five in the morning until late into the evening, was crippling and began to affect his health as it did to many local farmers. He decided to give up on dairying and go into beef, and now he raises some 190 Limousin and Angus beef cattle on his own eighty acres and a rented fifty, from which he also harvests hay for sale to horse owners, as well as contracting on other farms.

But the wind is unrelenting. Our conversation has had to be held at a social distance in the yard and, despite the welcome hot cup of tea, I'm chilled to the bone and bid farewell. I'll see Angie at the Dungworth choir practice when we can hopefully resume our singing sessions once more.

— 4 —

Outlaws of Loxley Common and the Chase

Not only books, but the story of the bare hills and woods themselves, and the transmitted memories of men tell us there was a real Robin o' th' Woods, who was an outlaw and forest robber. If that is so, then in all probability Hallamshire was his birthplace, for tradition says he was Robert of Loxley, a village at the Sheffield end of the ridge of Kirk Edge.

JOHN DERRY, THE STORY OF SHEFFIELD, 1910

January 27th 2020, Loxley Common.

This is such a fascinating place that I can't believe that it's taken me so long to discover it. This is not the case for many other people; the car parking area at the top of Long Lane is full even on a blustery Monday morning. Beside the carpark stands a massive old goat willow, its limbs, like reaching arms, splayed out along the ground as if it's exhausted, have rooted. Fresh shoots sprout from them, the tree having discovered the secret of immortality. In the tree's wide branches someone has hung bird feeders, freshly filled with goodies that are attracting waves of blue tits and great tits, as well as a couple of marauding grey squirrels, and in the topmost branches cling half a dozen rooks, all facing into the stiff wind, their black feathers ruffled. Two bunches of fresh flowers have been carefully laid on a wooden bird table nearby, in memory.

From the top of the ridge here, above the village of Loxley, the valley is laid out like a quilt. On the opposite side of the valley Stannington creeps along the ridge, looking remarkably like a Tuscan hill village. The three brown '60s multistorey blocks are fancifully reminiscent of the towers of San Gimignano. To the right the view takes in the full length of the valley, whilst in the opposite direction, from the far end of the spur, Sheffield's city centre emerges between the hills and valleys. Sheffield, for all its charms, is not a city of wide skies. Down in the valleys and on the hillsides lie most of the built-up areas and the horizons are narrow. Up here it's different and I inhale deeply, almost as though I'd been holding my breath for days.

It quickly becomes clear why the common is so popular this morning as I realise that I'm the only visitor minus a dog, or two, or several, and the dog bin is overflowing with plastic bags! The Common stretches towards the east, occupying the end of the ridge and forming a spur between the Loxley and Don Valleys. The top is quite flat, and is described on the website of the Loxley and Wadsley Commoners as 'an unusual area of heathland', but it's far more complicated than that. On both sides the land drops away steeply into deeply wooded hillsides. Much of the heathland is quite open, with paths through the heather and bilberry, but the commoners are concerned that this valuable habitat will be irrevocably lost under an invasion of birch and oak so they organise regular forays to beat them back. The removal of a number of larger trees has caused some local controversy. The importance of preserving the rich mix of habitats, however, is evidently demonstrated by the fact that the dedicated volunteers have recorded eighty-seven species of birds, including such rarities as nightjar and merlin, twenty-two species of butterfly and an extraordinary seventy-one species of moth on the Common.

Here and there stand old oaks of a most curious and locally distinctive shape. At some stage they have been coppiced to provide timber for tool handles and pit props so they have a squat rounded shape, with dozens of branches fanning from a wide base. In places the birches have taken possession and their closely packed white trunks shoot from mossy hummocks, casting long shadows in the bright winter sun, creating a slightly spooky alien landscape; a suitable set for an episode of *Doctor Who* or *Star Trek* maybe.

The heath falls away so steeply towards Loxley village that it has been named 'Loxley Edge.' Masses of huge angular boulders lie in no particular order but jumbled this way and that, between which stunted and gnarled oaks emerge. It's a landscape inherited from mining and quarrying. How many local grindstones, gateposts and horse troughs were laboriously hewn over the years from these rocks I wonder? Further down into the wood there are dips and openings that show where adits, coal and gannister mines, were driven into the rock face, and a wide hollow running down towards Loxley shows the route of a tramway where horses drew the corves full of gannister to the village.

The Eccentrics of Loxley House

Despite this area being known as a common, it has not always been in public hands. Although it is a small part of the former extensive mediaeval common lands of Wadsley and Loxley, under the Parliamentary Enclosure Act of 1784, it was placed in private ownership, and in 1795 the Reverend Thomas Halliday, the Unitarian minister for Norton, bought fifty acres at the edge of the common on which he built Loxley House, an imposing building standing today at the head of a drive off Ben Lane, Loxley. While at Norton he had married Martha Patrick, a lady of considerable wealth which enabled him to fulfil various ambitious projects that he had in mind, including the construction of a visitor attraction and tea house down in the valley bottom.

In 1808 Halliday sold the house to Thomas Payne of Wath, with 190 acres of land. In 1826 Payne completely rebuilt Loxley House as we see it today. The Paynes were Quakers, a family of successful South Yorkshire businessmen and farmers who were to own the common and the Loxley House estate for more than a hundred years. They began to exploit the mineral wealth of the common, leasing out the rights to the gannister mines and quarries. Large quantities of building stone were removed and most of the common was undermined with extensive workings.

The last member of the Payne family to live at Loxley House was the eccentric Dr Henry Payne who took up residence in the 1860s. He fell out with the local populace and the vicar of the nearby Wadsley Parish Church over a right of way across Wadsley Common which was part of Dr Payne's estate. So virulent was the dispute with the vicar that Payne said he would never go to church again. The parson reminded him he would be carried in at the end of his days, head first, in a coffin. But the determined doctor left instructions that he was to be buried on his own estate without a church ceremony and he marked the spot where he was to be buried with a stone, stating he wanted to be placed within a brick vault covered with earth in the plantation adjoining Loxley House. He even stipulated who should make his coffin, and of what wood, and named the gravediggers and the fee they were to receive! His unorthodox wishes were duly carried out in 1895.

The daughters of Dr Payne's sister Sarah inherited the properties after he died on 26th April 1895, and decided to gift seventy-five acres to the City of Sheffield, despite the fact that it was outside the city boundary at the time. The space became a very popular recreation area, visited by thousands of people on the weekends following the presentation. David Wragg, tenant of the Cave House, was appointed part-time keeper at a weekly wage of 6 shillings, with a uniform cap and coat.

At the same time, in 1895, the sisters sold Loxley House to Alderman William Clegg. Clegg was leader of the Sheffield City Council for many years and became Lord Mayor of Sheffield in 1898 although his local celebrity was based on him having played football for Sheffield Wednesday in the 1870s and making two appearances for England. He became known as the 'Uncrowned King of Sheffield' and he was knighted in 1906. Curiously enough Clegg is not the only professional footballer associated with the Loxley Valley. Two others, Cecil Coldwell, who played right-back for Sheffield United from 1951 to 1968, and Tony Hawksworth, who played as a goalkeeper for Manchester United, came from Dungworth. Hawksworth became one of only five players to win three consecutive FA Youth Cup winner's medals, in 1954, 1955 and 1956 and played international football for England at schoolboy and youth level.

In 1919 Loxley House was taken over by the remarkably politically incorrectly named Cripples Aid Association and later, when I knew it, was used by the Sheffield Sea Cadet Corps as a base. I could never understand this as Sheffield is about as far away from the sea as you can get in England! In 1996 the house was put up for sale and was bought by the property developers Campbell Homes who have turned it into luxury flats and apartments.

Murder at the Cave House

Thomas Halliday, as well as building Loxley House, had built a small house on his land tucked into Loxley Edge. It was known as the 'Cave House' because, although from the front it looked relatively normal, its rear room occupied a natural opening in the rock face. In 1812 it was the scene of a tragic and gruesome event. The house at this time was occupied by the local game keeper called Lomas Revill and his wife, Mary. It is said that, on the evening of 30th December 1812 the gamekeeper did not return home. As the hours passed a snowstorm swept across the common, until the landscape was shrouded in a thick mantle of white. The following day was New Year's Eve, and as morning broke, cold but fine, an acquaintance from nearby Wadsley called to exchange the compliments of the day with the dwellers in the lonely cottage. The visitor knocked and knocked again, but getting no response she tried the latch and finding the door would open, entered the room. Mary Revill lay on the floor, cold, in a pool of blood whilst in the cradle near the body the baby lay fast asleep.

Although her husband hadn't come home that night, footprints in the snow leading from the cottage seemed to enter a cave on the brow of the ridge and disappear. Strangely, as far as could be discerned, there were no footprints leading out of the cave. When the news of this terrible crime spread around the neighbouring hamlets there was much speculation. Who was the murderer? What was the mystery of the footprints?

Following a search Lomas Revill was discovered in a gamekeeper's cabin in the woods. Though he had been seen earlier in the evening in the village inn, much the worse for drink, no one could swear that the gamekeeper hadn't spent the night in the cabin. The murder remained a mystery but, as time went by, Lomas Revill became a strange man, prematurely aged with white hair, even though he was only forty-two years old. As New Year's Eve approached some years later, someone at the local inn remarked that the gamekeeper hadn't been seen for a few days. A party of men went up to the cottage on the common and there, in an outbuilding, found his body hanging from a rafter. The spectre of a white lady is said the haunt the area still. The Cave House, incidentally, was demolished using explosives in the 1920s.

Robin of Loxley

There is a proposal to erect a statue of Robin Hood in Loxley. A Sheffield sculptor, Anthony Bennett, well-known for producing some very curious works, has been commissioned to create the statue to stand on Loxley village green. He has so far created a small model which, it is hoped, will become a large bronze on a granite ball totalling an imposing twelve feet in height. It will show Robin of Loxley in a hollow tree as a twelve-year-old, the age it is said he was when he murdered his stepfather and became an outlaw and then hid in the nearby woods, aided by his mother. I'm all in favour of the project whether there is any true local connection with the outlaw or not. After all, the legend of Robin Hood is one of the most enduring of our national folk tales and his character is recognised right round the world.

I was once in a school in a run-down, all-black area of downtown Baltimore in the U.S. as part of a research project on raising school standards and I sat down next to a ten-year-old boy who was sitting with his head in a reading book. I tentatively approached him in what I hoped was a friendly manner, and asked him what the book was about. He slid the open pages across the desk and there was a picture of Robin Hood in his usual medieval guise, bow and arrow poised. It was so incongruous that I did a double take. "Well," I said, "do you know, I come from the place that Robin Hood comes from?" The child turned his head slowly and simply looked at me quizzically as though I had come from a different planet, which, in a way, I had.

If you have ever heard of Loxley it's probable that it's in connection with the legend of Robin Hood; Robin of Locksley. Even so it's a fair bet that you never associated the Locksley of Robin Hood with the valley in Sheffield. How is it then that this enduring myth has arisen? Is this a spurious claim to fame or is there some foundation for it? After all, Loxley is miles away from Sherwood Forest and the Sherriff of Nottingham certainly never had jurisdiction here. The claim, however, that Robin Hood originated from the Loxley Valley is one which has a long history and, despite there being not a shred of real historical evidence to support it, plenty of writers have lent their support to the legend and the 'Loxley and Wadsley Commoners' have now taken it to their hearts. Sheffield editor and Alderman, John Derry included a whole chapter entitled 'The Woodland Hero of Hallamshire' in his 1910 book for schools *The Story of Sheffield* in which he stated that *"The evidence is strong that the genuine Robin Hood was a Hallamshire man"* before failing to actually offer any.

The first mention of an association with Loxley seems to have been made in an anonymous Tudor manuscript in the Sloan collection in the British Library which retells the familiar legend, adding simply that Robin's birthplace was 'Locksley'. This supposed local association of the villain with our locality was strengthened by John Harrison, the surveyor who was charged in 1637 with the responsibility of recording all the properties and belongings that the Duke of Norfolk had inherited through his recently becoming Lord of the Manor of Sheffield. This he did in intricate and thorough detail in his *Exact and Perfect Survey and View of the Manor of Sheffield*, probably the most important historical document in Sheffield's archive. In this document Harrison, in listing the Duke's properties in Loxley, allows himself to stray from his remit a little, for against the listing for a piece of land in Loxley village called 'Little Haggas Croft' he adds, *"wherein is ye foundacion of a house or cottage where Robin Hood was borne."* He also mentions a place referred to as 'Robin Hood's Bower' in nearby Ecclesfield. Would, oh would, that we could go back and ask Harrison where he had gleaned this historical nugget, for, as it is well to remember, this entry was written at least 400 years after the supposed outlaw roamed the land.

Other historians, including the noted antiquarian and historian of all things pertaining to Yorkshire, Roger Dodsworth, writing about the same time, and in all probability referring to the same evidence, further embroidered the legend:

> Robert Locksley, born in Bradfield Parish, in Hallamshire, wounded his step father to death at plough; fled into the woods, and was relieved by his mother till he was discovered. Then he came to Clifton on Calder, and became acquainted with Little John, that kept the kine; which said John is buried at Hathersage in Derbyshire, where he hath a fair tombstone with an inscription.

In the early nineteenth century the celebrated local historian of Hallamshire, Joseph Hunter was able, in his position as Assistant Keeper of Public Records at the National Archives, to turn his attention to researching the derivation of the Robin Hood legend. He sought to confirm the historical authenticity of the characters that appeared in the early 'Rhymes' and 'Gest' of Robin Hood that had been familiar to people from the fourteenth century onwards. In doing so he identified a Robyn or Robert Hood in the year 1324 as one of his porters when Edward II made a circuit of the Royal Forests of Yorkshire and Nottingham. Hunter then identified a Robert Hood of Wakefield who was outlawed and executed by Edward for rebellion whose story bore some parallels to that of the Robin in the stories. He was not, however, able to connect the two and concluded;

This appears to me to be, in all likelihoods, the outline of his life; some parts of it however have a stronger claim to our belief than other parts. It is drawn from a comparison of the minstrel testimony of records of different kinds and lying in different places.

Hunter is referring to the fact that before the end of the fifteenth century Robin and his so called 'Merry Men' had become very familiar as characters in plays acted out in the May Games and he suggests that it was the echo of these performances themselves that was being perpetuated in the localities that bear their memory. As Hunter says;

We hear of this person and the other being the veritable Robin Hood and Little John, and houses are shown where they lived, and graves where they are interred. All these stories may safely be referred to this; that these are traditionary recollections, not of the veritable heroes themselves, but of persons who sustained those characters in the dramatic entertainments which were founded on the story, and who attained a celebrity for the ability with which they performed the parts.

The reference to 'Robin Hood's Bower' lends weight to this explanation for such bowers were a feature of the popular May Games, which all suggests that the people of Loxley in the sixteenth century would have enjoyed the annual visit of the guisers and mummers performing the jests and sword fights in the traditional tale. In 1893, however, Samuel Addy, the inveterate searcher into local superstitions, folk tales and traditions, suggested a quite different origin for Loxley's 'Haggis Croft' having been associated with Robin Hood. *"We can be almost sure"*, he states in *The Hall of Waltheof*, *"that Haggas Croft was once the abode of a sorceress or witch who used the familiar name of Robin for the wood sprite whose aid she was trying to invoke!"* Hmm..

A friend of mine, the artist and folk musician Robin Garside, who lives in Loxley, is of the opinion that the legend of Robin Hood as we know it today, having been embroidered through the centuries, is a classic folk tale spun from a number of real life events and characters. Meanwhile a teacher at Loxley Primary School, Archaeological Sciences graduate Dan Eaton, has received considerable local newspaper coverage for his claims that the woodland behind the school shows evidence of being of a considerable age and he points to this location as the 'Haggas Croft' of the early records. So the embroidery continues.

And, just as I thought that I'd exhausted my exploration of the legend of Robin Hood, a new strand of evidence was offered by two researchers, David Pilling and Rob Lynley, who, whilst digging in the Public Records Office at Kew, discovered the following amongst the entries in the 'Roll of King's Pardons' for 1382, during the reign of Richard II; *"Robert Hode otherwise known as Robert Dore of Wadsley given the King's pardon on 22nd May 1382,"* suggesting that the outlaw had been involved in the riots in York over the previous two years.

I'm going to leave the last word on the subject to James Holt, Professor of Medieval History at Cambridge University who, following his thorough researches into the archives for his book on the subject concludes that;

> Robin Hood is a legend rather than a man. The legend began more than six hundred years ago. The man, if he existed at all, lived even earlier. He has survived as a hero in ballad, book, poem and play ever since. He cannot be identified.

Frank Fearn, the Murderer

Despite being a relatively sparsely populated area, the Loxley Valley seems to have suffered more violent deaths than could have reasonably been expected, including a number of murderous attacks. One of the most celebrated and cold-blooded must be that of the murder of the watchmaker Nathan Andrews by Frank Fearn in 1782. The Fearn family lived at Hill Farm, just over the northern edge of the valley, but had fallen on hard times. Frank Fearn worked as a filesmith and was known as a pretty rough character.

At some stage Fearn had concocted a plan to make some cash by tricking a watchmaker to accompany him to a lonely spot, murder him and steal his stock of watches. He had therefore called on a well-known watchmaker who had a shop in Sheffield High Street, called Nathan Andrews, to ask him to go with him to Bradfield, where a number of gentlemen had got together to form a 'watch club', a sort of savings club in which each member in turn would be able to buy a watch. Andrews told him that it wasn't worth his while until there were enough members but as soon as there were twenty members in the club he would be pleased to go up to Bradfield to meet them and show them a selection of watches.

It wasn't long before Fearn was back and told Andrews that the club now had twenty members and so, early on the afternoon of March 18th 1782 they set out together, Fearn in his working clothes and Andrews in white stockings, short black gaiters, black breeches, waistcoat and hat. It was a long walk and we are left to wonder how Fearn managed to persuade Andrews to proceed with the venture, especially as it would be dark on his return journey. By the late afternoon they had reached the road to Bradfield at Kirk Edge, on the wilds of Loxley Common. Here, in this secluded spot, they were alone. Fearn pulled a pistol from his pocket and shot Andrews in the back. He followed this up by taking out a knife and stabbing him several times before beating out his brains with a fencing stake. He then removed the watches and high-tailed it back to his lodgings on Hawley Croft in Sheffield.

Later that evening a young man called Wood discovered the body and realised from the clothing that it was the same man that he had seen with Fearn, with whom he was acquainted, the same afternoon. The alarm was raised, Fearn was arrested the next day and the stolen watches discovered in his room. He was sent to York for trial, found guilty and sentenced to hang. This was all very dreadful but it was what happened next that makes this case such a celebrated one locally, for the judge, Mr Justice Eyre, wishing to make an example of the murderer and a warning to others issued the following order:

I do hereby order that the execution of Francis Fearn be respited until Tuesday 23rd of July and that his body, instead of being anatomised, shall be afterwards hanged in chains on a gibbet, to be erected on some conspicuous spot on Loxley Common at a convenient distance from the highway

and some weeks later a York newspaper reported that:

Last Tuesday was executed at Tyburn, near this city, Francis Fearn for the murder of Mr Nathan Andrews, watchmaker of Sheffield. He behaved with great fortitude and resignation, acknowledged the justice of his sentence and died duly penitent.

The body of Fearn was accordingly transported from York in a specially constructed iron cage. Thomas Holdsworth was paid 15 shillings to erect the post on Kirk Edge and a crowd gathered to watch as the cage was hoisted onto the hook. If the engraving that was made of the occasion is a true representation of the event, it was like a gala day with tents, flags and all the paraphernalia of a good day out. The gruesome, caged body was to swing in the wind for the next 15 years! It was not until Christmas Day 1797 that Fearn's decomposing skeleton finally fell from its cage.

For many years to come the sight of the gibbet post would instil fear and dread amongst travellers and it is said that few people would cross the common at night for fear of Fearn's ghost. The Sheffield writer Samuel Roberts refers to this in a story called 'Tales of the Poor' in 1829 in which his hero, Charles, was travelling to Bradfield:

Bradfield was about five miles distant. The whole way lay over one of the highest, roughest and least frequented moors in the neighbourhood. Charles, however, was acquainted with every rock and every cavern. He took the road over Loxley Edge, the highest ridge of the moors. He had to pass beneath the bleached bones of the murderer Frank Fearn which hung swinging in the gibbet in the almost decayed iron rings that once contained his body. He could not but shudder when he saw, by the transient glare of the flashes of sheet lightening which at times illuminated the atmosphere, the skeletal remains of the treacherous and ferocious murderer Fearn swinging above his head, as threatening every moment to fall and crush him to death on the very spot where the unoffending Andrews had perished.

The Convent of the Holy Ghost

A little further along the breezy ridge, at a spot known as 'Kirk Edge', with the Loxley Valley on one side and Oughtibridge on the other, is a small group of sombre institutional-looking buildings, surrounded by dark conifers and a high wall. It is locally known simply as 'The Convent'. In 1871 the Roman Catholic Duke of Norfolk, Henry Howard, had provided eighteen acres of his surrounding moorland in this inhospitable spot where, almost 100 years earlier, the murdered body of Nathan Andrews had been discovered in a copse across the road, and financed the construction of an orphanage for 300 Roman Catholic children. This original plan was never brought to fruition and the building that now houses the Convent actually opened in 1875 as an industrial school for girls who had been placed under the care of the Sisters of Charity of St Vincent de Paul by the courts for reasons such as vagrancy or because they were deemed of being in 'moral danger'. Inspection reports were positive about their care, saying that the girls were treated with kindness but it must have been a pretty grim institution, for the girls had to work by taking in and doing laundry to help pay for their keep. An area of the surrounding moorland had been taken in and five cows were kept. The girls were certainly out of the way of 'moral danger' way up here! By 1880 there were about seventy girls housed here, rising to over 100 by 1884, but the laundry proved to be an inappropriate form of occupation for them as the building stands high atop the ridge, and supplying a consistent flow of water proved extremely problematic. There was no mains water to the building and water had to be pumped from the valley below by a windmill. This proved to be completely impractical and so in 1887 the occupants were transferred to St. Joseph's at Walkley and the building closed.

It stood empty for a while before becoming for a short time a reformatory for boys. Rather curiously it was used to house a number of boys who were sent there after burning the boat called *The Clarence* on the River Mersey, on which they had been housed. In 1905, however, the boys were transferred to a new school in Widnes, and the Duke of Norfolk, at the suggestion of his sister, presented the building and land to the Catholic Church for use as a monastery by the world-wide 'Reformed Order of Discalced Carmelites', a very strict and austere order, first created in the twelfth century, and then re-established in the sixteenth century by St. Teresa of Avilla. 'Discalced' incidentally, is derived from Latin, meaning 'without shoes'. The building needed considerable alterations. A new chapel was built the surrounding wall was raised from fifteen to twenty feet to ensure total seclusion. On the 16 July 1911 it was consecrated as 'The Convent of The Holy Ghost'. It is now one of eleven such 'Carmels' in England. Inside is a Sacred Enclosure, which is cut off entirely from the rest of the building, so sacred that the only people allowed inside are the sisters, the Bishop of the Diocese, and the reigning Sovereign.

During the 1914–18 war Miss Phyllis Browne, daughter of the Rector of Bradfield Church, and teacher at High Bradfield School, having lost her fiancée in action, entered the Convent, taking the White Veil. Each Sunday friends visited her but were only allowed to converse through a small double grill. Sometime later Miss Browne left the Convent and married. She ended her days in Bridlington in the 1970s.

Today there are eleven Carmelite nuns at what is now called 'The Monastery of The Holy Spirit'. On Monday 5 October 2009, the monastery was honoured to host the relics of Saint Thérèse of Lisieux for three hours as part of a nationwide tour of the UK. At the time, Sister Mary of the Resurrection, aged eighty-three and prioress of the monastery, stated: *"We were surprised but very privileged to be chosen, we thought the relics would go to the Cathedral in Sheffield. It's a big event for us and a joy."* BBC Radio Sheffield's reporter Kate Linderholm visited the Relics, reporting:

It's quite a strange atmosphere. The roads have been closed – it's out in a beautiful stretch of countryside. As you get closer you can hear the sound of singing. Several hundred people are waiting patiently in line. There are big coaches arriving. They've come from all over to be here and look at these relics. I've never seen anything like this and I've never known an atmosphere like it.

In these days and weeks that we are confined during the coronavirus outbreak 'Lockdown', I can't help thinking of the people that have been confined here, including the women who today spend their whole lives behind these dour walls in such severe self-imposed isolation.

5

Dissenters and Nonconformists

There is a non-conformist got into one of the chapels of the Parish of Bradfield, either at Stannington or Midhope, encouraged by Mr Marriot, one of the burgesses of Stannington,

ARCHBISHOP SHARPE, 1700.

February 27th 2020, Bowcroft Quaker Burial Place

Above Stannington, on the high ridgeline that divides the Loxley and Rivelin valleys, the sky is clearest blue for the first time in weeks but the wind is absolutely biting. To the west the high moorlands are white with a light covering of snow that fell during the night. Above the field beside the road a pair of lapwings is already into their springtime courtship display, screaming and mewing, wheeling and swooping in an exuberant aerobatic display, pied wing patterns flashing in the bright sunlight. Despite the cold they give hope that the grey, wet winter may be turning the corner.

On the left of the road is a stone walled enclosure surrounded by trees. A narrow squeeze gives access through the wall and an engraved stone plaque beside it explains to visitors that this place is *'Bowcroft Cemetery, Ancient Quaker Burial Ground, wherein lie the remains of the Shaw family of Hill and Brookside.'* It seems very curious that a graveyard should house the remains of just one family but this is the case, for lying in the grass are some six or seven large engraved gravestones, mostly broken in two, all bearing the same surname, the largest of which reads:

HERE LIES

THE BODY OF

GEORGE SHAW

LATE OF BROOKE-SIDE

WHO DEPARTED

THIS LIFE ON THE 5th

DAY OF THE 5th MO

1708 IN THE 75th

YEAR OF HIS AGE

HE SUFFERED MUCH

FOR BEARING HIS

TESTIMONY AGAINST

THE PAYMENT OF

TYTHES

Nearby, similar stones record the burial places of George's brother William of 'Hill' and the brothers' wives Fines and Frances. 'Hill' and 'Brookside' are farms that still face each other on the slopes leading down into the valley.

The Shaws were a prominent Quaker family that lived at these two farms in the seventeenth and eighteenth centuries, at a time when Quakers were persecuted. The family must have had some significance in the early development of the Quaker faith in the whole region because in 1678 William Shaw arranged a meeting at Hill farm for George Fox, the Quaker founder. Believing that the path to God is a personal one and not through the ministrations of a paid priest, they refused to pay their tithes, a tenth part of their income, which was used to support the clergy and church of the parish, in this case Ecclesfield Parish. The brothers were relentlessly pursued for their tithes. When they couldn't or wouldn't pay, George and William were eventually prosecuted by the Prior of Ecclesfield and imprisoned in York Castle prison in 1698 for five years and five months. They were both over seventy when finally released. Both brothers had a previous history of prison. In 1661 they had both spent time in Derby Jail for attending a Quaker meeting in Eyam. As Quakers they were not permitted to be buried in the parish graveyard when they died so in 1675 the two brothers, George and William Shaw, had purchased this plot of land above Stannington for their family burial ground, and here, in this peaceful spot, their broken gravestones still lie.

Curious tales are told in connection with the cemetery. Mr Jack Goodison told the story of a farmer of Brookside Farm who thought that the ancient gravestones would make excellent cold slabs for his dairy. He loaded the stones accordingly onto a dray and four horses pulled the load down to Brookside. Strangely, however, whenever milk was placed to cool on the slabs it curdled. Eventually the farmer decided to return the stones to the cemetery and it was said that only one horse was required for the return trip up the hill!

If Bowcroft is one of the oldest burial sites in the valley, directly across the road a brand-new sign announces the newest, the Bradfield View Woodland Burial Site, created so recently that there have been no customers yet. There had been some opposition when the plans were publicised in 2018 and Bradfield Parish Council initially objected to the proposal but permission was granted in 2019 and work has started to prepare the site. Fourteen areas will be laid out accommodating between 400 and 500 plots, each marked with the planting of a tree or a small memorial stone, and informal paths will weave through the flower rich grassland. The view across the valley is incomparable. Personally I can't imagine a more wonderful place to be buried.

June 9th 2020, Underbank

From the windy ridge above Stannington a footpath leads through the future burial site and across the open access land at the top of the hillside that is known as 'The Griffs'. The last time I was up here was in February on a cold, clear day but now, in June, it's very different. The hillside is one long hay meadow with golden buttercups and ox-eye daisies shooting through the tall feathery grasses. A gate at the bottom joins an old packhorse way, lined with foamy cow parsley, tall sycamores and oaks and a tumbled stone wall, against which purple foxgloves stand erect. Swallows and house martins swoop and glide between the trees, chaffinches sing for all they're worth and a charm of goldfinches twitter in the wayside gorse bushes. Across the valley the haymaking is in progress and the rectangular chessboard of fields on Loxley Common is a patchwork quilt of greens and yellows. Summer is reaching its height, the perfect moment before things start to go over in the heat.

The track leads down to join the main road between Stannington and Dungworth at an acute angle and here stands a plain rectangular building with symmetrically arranged windows with rounded tops. High on the gable wall a stone plaque tells us that this was the 'Day and Sunday School, Erected in 1853'. On the opposite side of the road, set amongst mature trees within the sloping fields that lead down to the river, surrounded by a well-tended graveyard, is a chapel of the most distinctive and sophisticated design. It is jewel of a building, quite unlike any other. The front facing the road has absolutely symmetrical features; two very tall round-headed windows with multiple small panes, and twin doors, originally for men and women, above which are circular 'oculus' windows. Underbank Chapel, as it is called, is the successor to an earlier place of worship that stood here from May 1652 that was built as a Chapel of Ease to St Nicholas, Bradfield, when a certain Richard Spoone of Stannington left in his will some properties in trust for the maintenance of a minister as well as a sum towards the paying for the teaching of poor children whose parents could not afford to keep them at school. A small congregation began to meet in a converted barn on an adjoining site to today's chapel.

Until the seventeenth century the spiritual needs of the people of the whole valley had been served exclusively by the medieval church high on the hill at Bradfield. By the end of the seventeenth century however there was a growing dissatisfaction with the established church and a strong streak of nonconformity flowed through the valley led by Quakers like the Shaws, closely followed by the Wesleyans, Methodists of various denominations and Unitarians. By the nineteenth century members of five different faith communities were practicing in the valley; the Anglicans, Roman Catholics, Quakers, Unitarians and Methodists, each with their own places of worship.

These were turbulent times of widely opposing religious views and Underbank chapel's early years were beset by controversy. In May 1662, the Act of Uniformity was passed ordering that worship everywhere should be conducted by the clergy strictly in accordance with the newly issued Book of Common Prayer, and that every minister should give a public declaration of 'unfeigned assent and consent' to its contents. This was not forthcoming from the minister here at Underbank and it's unclear whether he had his licence withdrawn or if he resigned. By about 1700 they had broken with the established church and counted themselves Dissenters. Within a few years the original chapel had become unfit for use and Thomas Marriott of Ughill Hall, a Calvinist dissenter, built the unusual and beautiful chapel that stands today. It was opened for worship on 2 June 1743.

In 1785 the chapel congregation made yet another change of denomination as it decided to embrace Unitarian beliefs. Underbank remains a Unitarian chapel today. Many of the congregation at the time, however, could not accept Unitarianism and left the church, either returning to St. Nicholas or attending the newly opened Congregational church on Queen Street in the centre of Sheffield.

In 1796 Underbank had a most unexpected and illustrious visitor; the poet and friend of Wordsworth, Samuel Taylor Coleridge, who at that time was considering becoming a Unitarian minister. He recorded his eventful walk over from Sheffield in his diary:

> I trudged thither over hill and dale thro' a worse road than ever Flibbertigibbet led poor Tom. ... it was now dark; and into pits and out of pits and against stones I contrived to stumble some mile and a half out of my way.

Stannington Charity Schools

The first school at Underbank was established shortly after Richard Spoone left a property called Sim House in his will dated 23 May 1652 *"for the education of poor children whose parents are willing but unable to keep them in school."*

As was the usual pattern of educational provision until the late nineteenth century, schooling in the valley was in the hands of religious bodies, and Ralph Wood, the minister of the chapel, was the first schoolmaster. He was paid 17/6d a quarter to teach seven poor pupils, though he undoubtedly would have taken others. In 1715 the endowment was increased when Thomas Marriot of Ughill left a bequest to enable the teaching of an additional seven or eight children.

But as time went on the records suggest that the teaching and learning must have been pretty rudimentary. An inspector reported in 1836 that *"The children are not taught writing, only reading and spelling, the master alleging that he had no instructions to teach writing."* The elderly teacher, who had taught here for the extraordinary length of time of forty-seven years, however, struggled on until 1844 by which time he was eighty-three years old! The school by this time was in a sorry state. It was reported that *"the windows were out of repair and the door in a shattered condition."*

In February 1844 George Revitt, aged twenty-one, was appointed master by the trustees, being paid an annual salary of £20, though out of this he was expected to pay for the building to be whitewashed once a year! He remained master for thirty-one years. Under him the school prospered so well that the trustees decided to demolish the old school and build a new one on the same site, the building that still stands opposite the chapel. It was opened on 8 May 1854 with a 'Public Tea Party, tickets one shilling and sixpence each'. Towards the end of his days at Underbank School, however, Revitt began to despair. Things were slow to improve and it was evidently an uphill struggle. In an out of the way rural community like this many parents were not only unable but also unwilling to send their children to school. He wrote in the Log Book in 1874: *"The children as a rule are very stupid and difficult to teach. Order very poor this week. Holiday given on account of there being a bazaar in the schoolroom."* Oh dear, we've all had weeks like that.

By the time the Rev. Alfred Moon took up the position as schoolmaster, although over seventy boys and girls between eight and thirteen were on the register, under a succession of apparently inexperienced teachers order and discipline were still a problem, and the deficiencies were highlighted in successive reports. The school suffered from the fact that it was by this time not the only school to which Stannington parents could choose to send their offspring. In fact it was one of four such schools, all provided by different religious denominations. Log book entries in 1876 indicate that *"a large number of children on the register as left by the previous master are marked absent but in reality have left the school,"* and *"Many children make the rounds of the schools before settling down at one particular one."* Despite this parents were not always supportive of their children's education. *"Parents will not send their children to school. Visited many of them and most say that their children are better scholars than they are and that they have had enough schooling."*

Things went from bad to worse. James Mawson, the new master who had taken over in 1876 summed up the position: *"The children are totally unfit for examination, are undisciplined, unpunctual, irregular in their payments and very unequal in their attainments."* He lasted only six months! His successor agreed: *"The higher classes have not the slightest idea of the words they read, the book language being entirely above their comprehension"* and noted that *"A great number of children between 5 and 7 are not attending any school."*

The log books and Inspection reports for the next twenty years make startling and distressing reading – in 1887: *"The master is much in need of assistance as he has to teach singlehandedly five standards"*; in 1893: *"The lack of ventilation (owing to the windows having been shut for the past twelve months) was so distressing that several panes of glass had to be broken by the teacher at the start of the inspection"*; and in 1906: *"The order in Standard IV is still very bad; the teacher seems to have quite lost control. No lesson has been given to my satisfaction in this class today. Books getting dirty stacked on the harmonium and fireplace as there is no cupboard. There are open fireplaces and no fireguards. I understand that children have had their dresses burnt."*

The weather in December 1909 was apparently exceptionally severe as the log book records: *"Children could not commence work on account of the ink being frozen. Several babies have cried with the cold."* Such a state of affairs could not be allowed to continue and in 1910 the new Stannington Council School, in which the local infants are still taught, was opened and Underbank Day School was closed.

Though the Dissenters had been educating local children at Underbank for over 250 years it was not until the early nineteenth century that the other denominations, the Methodists, Anglicans and Roman Catholics opened their own schools in the area. The first were the Methodists who opened a Sunday School attached to the new Knowle Top Methodist Church in 1822 but it was the Anglicans, who opened their Church School in 1829, following the opening of the new Parish Church at Stannington, who were the first to offer an alternative day school. By 1844 110 children; forty boys and ten girls as well as sixty infants, were registered.

Dungworth School, where my grandchildren now attend, began as a church school in 1837 but was reopened as a National School in 1876. Inspectors reported: *"The school has lately established in a wild, outlaying district. The school is very backward and the children, especially the younger ones, are not under control."* The school had the usual problems of poor attendance, especially at harvest and blackberrying time, and in April 1880 the headteacher wrote that the bell could not be rung *"hence the children have no way of knowing the proper times of opening the school."* Presumably there were no clocks in their homes. Other entries in the school log books reflect the living conditions of the time. An entry In September 1890 relates that *"Horace Hawksworth, a good little boy in standard 1, died of Diptheria; this complaint is fearfully bad in the area, 17 cases known amongst the children."*

In 1871 the Methodist Sunday School was reopened as 'Stannington Mixed School' and by 1875 there were 109 children on their books. Whilst the little schools established by the charitable bodies closed in the early 1900s the charming buildings still stand, helping to chart the shaky development of the education system that our children enjoy today.

May 28th 2020, Loxley Chapel

A walk of a mile takes me down an ancient footpath beside Underbank Chapel, called Spoon Lane, to cross the Loxley at Rowel Bridge and up the other side of the valley to Loxley Road. On the opposite side of the road, behind wrought iron gates and through an avenue of ancient hollies stands what remains of Loxley Chapel. The contrast between the spick-and-span Underbank Chapel on the opposite side of the valley and Loxley Chapel, its mirror image on this side, is stark despite both having been erected during the eighteenth century. I have visited the graveyard that surrounds the old building many times to see the gravestones of the flood victims that are buried here but never have I seen it in such a state. Even Sleeping Beauty's princely rescuer would have his work cut out to hack through the tangle of brambles and undergrowth that has entirely engulfed it. The architecturally important, Grade 2 listed building, one of the only eighteenth century church buildings in the city, stands in complete ruin. All the interior fittings are completely destroyed and the roof is gone. Only the stone outer walls still stand, a shell of a building, the window openings devoid of glass. It's a tragic sight, and the circumstances leading to its present condition are even more tragic.

Only the few tallest Victorian monuments that emerge from the vegetation give an indication that the graveyard exists at all. Hidden here, however, are a number of the graves and poignant memorials of families who drowned in the Loxley Valley flood of 1864. Some are inscribed with the sort of sanctimonious doggerel beloved of the Victorians. That of six members of the Price family from Malin Bridge has:

Like crowned forest trees we stand, and some are marked to fall,
The axe will strike at God's command, and soon shall smite us all.

The extraordinary memorial verse on the gravestone of Ann Mount, who was swept out of her shop at Malin Bridge, is remarkably down to earth in its tone;

Sudden the Gush, T'was thus she fell,
Not even time to bid her friends farewell.

The gravestone of seventeen-year-old Elizabeth Crownshaw, a servant at the Stag Inn at Malin Bridge, who had only started to work there a few days before the disaster, bears the inscrutable inscription:

The Rose in its beautiful bloom,
The sun's brightest glories decline;
So early came I to the tomb,
Repent lest the case should be thine.
The busy tribes of flesh and blood,
With all their cares and fears,
Are carried downward by the flood,
And lost in following years.

But this is not the only stone here that records lives lost at 'The Stag'. The most striking and tragic memorial anywhere to victims of the flood is the huge, rounded gravestone of the Armitage family that stands almost six feet tall behind the chapel. Sixty-seven-year-old Eliza Armitage was the landlady. Her son William, his wife and five children, her other son, Greaves, his wife and their two children, are all remembered here, though the bodies of four of the children were never recovered. I begin to push through the twining briers and nettles but it's impossible to get near enough to make out whether or not it's still standing.

The building of this new chapel came about following a further rift within the congregation of St Nicholas in 1787 when John Webster was appointed curate. Many of the Bradfield congregation were unhappy as he was also curate of St. Swithin's, Holmesfield, way away on the opposite side of Sheffield, and never actually lived in Bradfield. They made it known that they preferred the deputy curate, Benjamin Greaves, who was about to be dismissed, to John Webster. When their wishes were not met, they decided to found their own chapel further down the valley towards Loxley, taking Benjamin Greaves with them. Ironically Greaves himself left in 1796 for a living in Stoney Middleton, only returning to Loxley for occasional services. Despite the church having been built for the use of the Established Church it ran into problems right from the start when the church authorities refused to consecrate the building for worship due to the fact that it did not incorporate an east-facing window, and it became known as the Loxley Congregational Chapel.

By 1798 the building was sold at auction for £315 to a group of Protestant Dissenters or Independents who changed its name to the Loxley Independent Church. From 1802 it had its own pastor, the Rev. Daniel Dunkerley under whom it thrived. According to the Religious Census of 1851 an average congregation at an afternoon service was 200. In 1855 a new school-room and minister's house was built. An entry in the baptism register records that in 1872 Henry Tingle Wilde, Chief Officer of the *Titanic*, was christened at the church! The chapel continued as a place of worship throughout the twentieth century, having yet another change of name to the 'Loxley United Reformed Church' in the 1970s. Its congregation, however, had dwindled and it was closed in 1993.

The building was purchased by a local contractor, Hague Farming of Bradfield, but was allowed to gradually deteriorate into a ruinous state. Despite efforts to keep the building secure vandals broke into the church, not to appreciate its fittings and memorials but to wreak destruction. Photographs of the interior that appeared in a feature article in the *Daily Mail* in 2015 are truly shocking. They show the chapel in an appalling state; the massive organ keyboard smashed, piles of rotting hymn books scattered over the floor, floorboards ripped up and the ceiling hanging down. It could, and should, still have been saved but, in the early hours of 17 August 2016, the church was set on fire. Three fire engines took hours to extinguish the blaze and the building was completely gutted. Only a shell remains. I regret that I never had the opportunity to see the interior of the chapel, with its polished wooden gallery and grand organ.

This may not, however, be the end of the story. In 2016 the ruins were purchased for £86,000, by Mr Mohammed Jameel Ali who wants to build a respite centre for disabled children in the grounds, which would be named in memory of his niece who tragically died aged just eight. Work has been carried out to stabilise the walls and secure the property and he and his architect are working with councillors and Historic England to draw up the proposals. A 'Friends' group has been created to help safeguard the chapel's future but I'm afraid that it's too late to save anything worthwhile. It is not too late, however, to save and restore the historically important graveyard that surrounds the chapel and its unique memorials to the victims of one of the greatest disasters of Victorian England.

A Church for Stannington

By the beginning of the nineteenth century, for those living in the growing township of Stannington, the trek of four miles to attend the parish church at Bradfield was becoming more and more inconvenient, especially in winter. They were therefore relieved when, in 1824 a grant of just less than £3000 was allocated from the national 'Million Fund', money voted by parliament as a result of the Church Building Act 1818, towards the building of a new parish church in Stannington. Because the funding was designed to provide new places of Anglican worship in the growing industrial towns it was highly unusual for such a church to be built in a rural location like this. Sheffield was to benefit from the same 'Million Act' funding with grants being made for the building of four of the town's largest churches: St George's in 1825; Christ Church, Attercliffe in 1826; St Philip's, Shalesmoor in 1828 and St Mary's, Bramall Lane in 1830.

The laying of the Stannington foundation stone, on 16th October 1828 by Thomas Richard Ryder, Vicar of Ecclesfield, appears to have been a major occasion for the village. A procession from the Peacock Inn, Knowle Top, was led by a band followed by the constables, the Children of the Sunday School, the Vicars of Ecclesfield and Sheffield, the Mayor of Doncaster, the architect, the gentry, the superintending committee and the Stannington Union Sick Society, and the Inhabitants. Afterwards the worthies were entertained while they took tea, by the village folk and schoolchildren who sang two hymns written by the Sheffield hymnwriter, James Montgomery. The church was consecrated as 'Christ Church, Stannington' on 20th July 1830, and its own separate parish was created in 1843.

Christ Church, like many of the 'Million Act' churches, is a curious looking edifice, basically a rectangular box with eight peculiar, slender castellated turrets rising from the corners and an ugly narrow crocheted bell tower rising uncomfortably on top of the front gable above the door. Kelly's Directory described the church as:

> A Gothic building of stone, consisting of a nave, north and south
> aisles and a western turret containing one bell. There are box pews
> from the back wall to within a few feet of the twin pulpits, just in
> front of the altar rail and galleries on three sides. The choir sits in the
> west gallery where the organ is installed.

There was originally seating for 1000 people but it was evidently pretty uncomfortable because in 1881 the church was closed for five weeks for repainting, repairs and the installation of a 'warming apparatus'. Even so, in 1919 the *Sheffield Weekly News* records rather harshly that:

> The church's interior can boast of no great beauty... The plain
> wooden gallery is all round the church and there is a cold barrenness
> which belongs to all churches which were built out of the Million
> Fund Scheme when beauty of architecture or beauty in any shape or
> form was a minus quality.

The two long side balconies, which went across the windows making the church very dark, were removed only in 1964!

Initially Christ Church did not have a vicar but used the Bradfield curate, Mr William Gill, who lived at Broomhead Hall where he supplemented his stipend of £50 pa by acting as tutor to the family. For six years he maintained his onerous responsibilities, taking morning services at Bradfield and evening services, christenings and burials at Stannington even though he appears to have had no transport and travelled between the churches on foot. It is hardly surprising that he resigned in 1836 when he was asked to perform a morning service at Stannington as well!

To solve the problem of the clergyman needing to travel between the churches, a parsonage and school were built and a new vicar, Samuel Carver, a Sheffield man who had recently married a Cambridge woman of some wealth, was appointed. Sadly Mr and Mrs Carver were both killed when their horse bolted causing their carriage to overturn at Malin Bridge. At which point, in 1846, a local petition asked the Vicar of Ecclesfield to allow the return of William Gill as Vicar. Accordingly he resigned his curacy of Bradfield and took services at Stannington and at the schools at Rivelin and Dungworth which were licensed for worship. In addition he taught pupils at the vicarage. In 1833 he married Ann Heywood and they had eight or nine children, only one surviving him. He and seven of his children are buried in the south east corner of the churchyard as are Mr and Mrs Carver.

Methodists

Whilst Quakerism had exerted a strong influence over a few of the valley's families during the late seventeenth and eighteenth centuries it was Methodism that took firm root amongst the valley's growing communities. In 1742 John Wesley had arrived in Sheffield on a preaching tour and founded the nucleus of the Sheffield Methodist Society. Following a shaky start, in which the first two of the society's meeting houses in the town were torn down by braying mobs, Methodism was quickly adopted and in 1780 the Norfolk Street Wesleyan Chapel was opened and consecrated by the seventy-seven-year-old John Wesley, who described it as *"one of the largest in the Kingdom."*

There is no record of John Wesley ever having visited Bradfield, however, and it was not until 1817 that the beautiful chapel on Mill Lee Road was built in Low Bradfield. It's built to a classically simple design, a plain rectangular preaching house with pleasingly large, symmetrical windows and a centrally placed doorway, all contrasting to the overblown gothic of the later chapel across the road that was built to replace it in 1899, funded by the Ibbotson family. They were generous benefactors of Low Bradfield, who gave the land for the cricket pitch and field that stands at the heart of the village, and they employed the esteemed Sheffield architect John Hale to indulge in a far more elaborate design for the new chapel than such a small village could otherwise have afforded. The first chapel then closed and now houses the Bradfield Parish offices and archives whilst the new chapel in turn closed in 1993 and is now a private residence, a similar fate that has been met by all of the Valley's chapels; Dungworth Ebenezer Chapel, built in 1850 and closed in 2017, Storrs Chapel built in 1884, and closed in 1975, and then, in late October 2020, Knowle Top Chapel, the most distinctive building in Stannington, the last of the valley's Victorian Methodist chapels which was built in 1821 and rebuilt in 1878, succumbed to falling membership and closed as a place of worship.

With the demise of the local chapels in the valley as elsewhere a whole way of life has died out within my lifetime. In a way that is becoming more and more difficult to imagine it was the nonconformist chapel in communities like this around which the life of the village revolved. In the valley as elsewhere, well within living memory, the yearly cycle was marked by customs and traditions linked to the churches' calendar, and in the community these were major events. I've been enjoying seeing a collection of old photographs that one of the older residents of Dungworth has been posting on Facebook. As well as featuring many of the long-standing families of the area, the Crappers, Hagues, Samworths and Dysons, they capture memorable moments and events in the village and they recall early memories of my own.

As a young child I attended Sunday school at our local Methodist chapel in Sheffield and have fond memories of the two or three annual events that we celebrated; the 'Anniversary', Harvest Festival and Whit Walks. The Anniversary (of what I never knew) service was held in May when the annual crowning of the May Queen took place. When I was eight years old I had the honour of being chosen as the attendant to the May Queen which entailed bearing a flowery crown on a satin cushion. Tiered wooden staging was set up in the chapel and we would learn songs like 'Jesus Wants Me for a Sunbeam' and 'Daisies are our Silver' to sing at the service. But the highlight of the day was the afternoon tea in the hall with meat paste sandwiches, jelly and buns. This was also the occasion on which the annual Sunday School prizes were distributed; children's books of Bible stories or tales of children who had borne trials and tribulations of one sort or another with courage and fortitude that even at this young age made me feel inadequate. A few weeks ago my mother died three days short of her 96th birthday and on clearing her house the other day I came across a collection of these inscribed awards that she had proudly treasured all these years.

Whitsuntide was the only regular occasion of the year that we had new clothes bought specially. All the chapel members, uniformed organisations and Sunday school in our best new outfits, would arrive early in the morning and form up in procession led by the Scout band behind a huge colourful banner, before setting off to join other such processions in Meersbrook Park, where a brass band led the massed singing of the assembled throng of hundreds. Later we were taken by coach to Chatsworth Park for races and a picnic.

Unfortunately I don't have any of the same sort of photographs of the Sunday School Anniversaries at our chapel as have been shared on the Valley internet site, where the similar local events were known as 'Sermons'. These wonderful images depict the rickety staging set up in Dungworth and Storrs with children on the top tier and the adults lower down, accompanied by a scratch orchestra. *"They were not connected with brass or silver prize bands. They were simply good quality local musicians – violins, cello and maybe a double bass plus organ"* adds one of the respondents on the Facebook page. These were events that involved the whole community and were held, not in the chapel unless it was very, very wet. The Dungworth Sermons, always held on the first Sunday in July, took place firstly in the yard of the butcher's shop then at Greenfold farmyard and then at Padley farm.

The regular calendar of these events at the eight or nine different chapels around the valley ensured that singers and musicians were able to augment each other's performances. The season began at Knowle Top, Stannington, on the Sunday before Whit Sunday, and carried on almost weekly to the final event at Loxley Methodist on the third Sunday in July. The musical skills of violinists, cellists, trombonists and double bass players were passed on through the generations and were honed at the weekly gatherings throughout the summer. Sam Elliott first played his fiddle at Storrs Sermon when he was eight years old and became the longest playing member and leader of the Dungworth orchestra. Charles Stenton was another violinist from Storrs who travelled the circuit for sixty-six years. The musician and folk singer Robin Garside remembers his father playing fiddle in the Dungworth orchestra, spawning his own lifetime interest in music. During the interwar years these events were at their peak but it was not until relatively recently that they faded away altogether. The last outdoor 'sermons' in Worrall was held in July 1961 but in Dungworth they lingered on until July 1981.

Dungworth, Sunday November 17th 2019

The date today may not be immediately notable to most people but, as it's the Sunday following Remembrance Day, it's a big day in the valley. Today the carol singing begins at the Royal. Approaching Dungworth the verges and roadside are already lined with cars so I find a parking space and hurry to the pub. It's 12.30 and as usual I've missed the start. From some way along the road the sound of raised voices in harmony already rings out as I approach. The Royal Hotel belies its name. It's in no way pretentious; in fact it's a bit scrappy which, to its dedicated band of customers, is much of its appeal. It's an old-fashioned village boozer, a local's pub with no airs and graces, that serves the valley community by providing a warm welcome and a great pint of Bradfield Bitter; and Linda's pies are to die for!

The pub windows are misted and as I open the door the wall of sound and the warm atmosphere welcomes me from the chilly morning air:

> At Jacob's Well, the stranger sought
> Her drooping frame to cheer, her drooping frame to cheer,
> Samaria's daughter little thought
> That Jacob's God was near.

The sing is already in full swing but advancing through the glass porch along the narrow corridor into the pub presents a problem. The whole place is already packed tight. I join in the next verse from the doorway, nodding to recognised acquaintances that meet every year only on these Sunday sings:

> This ancient well, no glass so true,
> Britannia's image shows, Britannia's image shows,
> Now Jesus travels Britain through
> But who the stranger knows?

As the final verse of this well-known local carol ends I begin to push through the assembled throng towards the bar. To the right I look over the half-glazed partition into the main room to where a familiar group in the middle, mainly men clutching pint glasses, are grouped around an electric organ at which a small lady, Sue Heritage, sits. Some of the singers are locals but there are other 'folky' regulars that I recognise as belonging to Sheffield morris and sword dance teams. To the left is a room with tables at which children sit colouring or playing on iPads. Dave, the landlord behind the bar, spots me amongst the crowd and has a pint of Bradfield Farmers Bitter waiting by the time I manage to reach it. It's busier than usual for the first sing but it will get even more packed during the next few Sundays up to Christmas when coach parties swell the numbers jammed in here to almost 200. As the organ starts up with the next tune (there's no announcements or introductions, everyone knows the words) I spot a couple of young guys with large cameras and recording equipment trying to manoeuvre the equipment through the crush. *"Channel 5 are recording for a programme sometime around Christmas,"* someone tells me. Three or four years ago someone visiting for the first time became alarmed at the overcrowding and raised the issue with the local council who, upon inspecting the premises, threatened to close it down as there was only one exit. The regular singers responded to the challenge and raised enough money to fund the construction of a new emergency exit beside the gent's toilet.

Sue sets off at a cracking pace with the introductory symphony to the next carol, *"While shepherds watch their flocks by night, All seated on the ground,"* it begins. Well, the words may be familiar but the tune for the uninitiated is certainly not. This one is called 'Pentonville', I've no idea why. It's one of my favourites amongst the thirty or so different versions of 'While Shepherds', four or five of which will be sung here today. The singing swells into a wall of sound in which it's impossible to hear yourself singing but it's not raucous, it's in harmony, most people singing either the tune or some version of the bass part. This works as most of these local carols have a fugal section in which one of the parts leads.

It's time for a solo and the customary call for order, *"Singer's on his feet"* – a strange injunction, considering that 90% of the singers are already standing. The familiar tall figure of Will Noble moves from propping up the bar to take up a position nearer to the organ. He's a stonewaller by trade and a well-respected local folk singer. Everyone knows what he's about to sing as the repertoire is always the same. *"The mistletoe hung on the old castle wall,"* he begins. It's a masterful rendition of the old ballad retelling a melancholy tale of a newlywed bride who accidentally locks herself in an old oak chest whilst playing hide-and-seek with members of her wedding party. Her desiccated body is discovered only years later. Everyone joins in the lugubrious last lines, *'Her bridal bloom lay withering there in a living tomb'.*

The session proceeds through versions of 'Wild Shepherds', 'The Holly and the Ivy', 'Star of Bethlehem', 'Hail Smiling Morn' and 'Behold the Grace Appears', all local favourites, interspersed with solos of 'Swaledale' and 'Stannington' rendered in a thin piping voice by an elderly soprano who has sung it for decades, and someone chimes up with 'Kris Kringle', *"Who comes this way, so blythe and gay, upon this merry Christmas Day,"* and the whole pub responds *"Ho ho, Ho ho, Ho ho, Ho ho, Kris Kringle with his Christmas tree."* It's an eclectic mix of traditional songs and carols.

The Royal in Dungworth is not the only place where this peculiar local carolling tradition takes place though it has become the most famous. The Blue Ball at nearby Worrall and the 'Top Red Lion' in Grenoside preserve similar unique traditions, each with their own repertoire and faithful followers and Stannington has its own robust tradition, maintained partly by the silver band. It is said that these carols, which can be traced in style to the seventeenth century Restoration, migrated into the public houses during the nineteenth century when the old 'west gallery' musicians were evicted in favour of the organ and the ancient carols replaced by the more demure Victorian versions that we know so well today.

The writer Thomas Hardy documented this movement in his fiction. From around 1801 his father and grandfather played stringed instruments in the church band at Stinsford, immortalised as 'Mellstock' in *Under the Greenwood Tree*. The accounts of the eviction of the Melstock Quire and their instruments and the similar fate of the Longpuddle musicians, who, following a long session on Christmas Eve absentmindedly broke into 'The Devil Among the Tailors' during the morning service, are particularly affectionate and sensitive. Very few of the old west gallery bands had survived by 1872 when *Under the Greenwood Tree* was published. The musical story of Bradfield Church mirrors that of Hardy's narrative. The church records show 5/- being allotted for a bass violin as late as 1838 but the musicians were replaced in 1842 by the organ, at a cost of £210 10s. In 1870 the galleries were taken down and the whitewash scrubbed from the walls in the course of a rigorous restoration of the building. It is not difficult to understand how it came to be that some of the old carols and carollers found a new home in the local hostelry. After all the old Ebenezer Chapel in Dungworth stands next door to the Royal!

This remarkable annual round of music making in the chapels and pubs has laid the foundation for a tradition in the valley that is very much alive today. Every Monday evening, I drive over to Dungworth for choir practice. It's a small community choir, only a dozen or so regulars, but we are able to produce a decent four-part rendering of the folk songs and local carols that form the core of our repertoire, and we are fortunate to have Jon Boden, the nationally regarded folk singer and musician who lives nearby, to lead us. Somehow the Village Hall contrives to be colder inside than the temperature outside but we soon get warmed up when we start singing. John also hosts the monthly folk club in the Royal where a couple of dozen folk aficionados are treated to a fairly intimate performance by some of the country's leading folk singers and musicians, attracted here by John's reputation and friendly persuasion, although it's the raffle that creates the most excitement!

For those straight-faced folk singers and musicians who take their music making 'seriously' the valley holds host to the annual 'Traditional Music Festival' which attracts artists from many parts of the country. It's organised by Mark Davies of Edgemount Farm, high above Bradfield. Mark is a larger-than-life character, a concertina player and collector, with many sides to his character. As well as being a first-tier immigration tribunal judge he was until recently also the chairman of the Barlow Hunt, a position which caused him the embarrassment of being arrested and tried for an alleged attack on hunt saboteurs last year. Although Mr Davies was acquitted of the offence the *Daily Mail* newspaper published a photograph which had appeared in a racy calendar, in which he is naked with only his concertina protecting his modesty. Beneath the picture the caption read: 'Would you like a squeeze?'

As a counterpoint to these 'low culture' musical activities the Valley can also offer opportunity for those of more highbrow tastes. For the last 23 years St Nicholas Church has been the venue for the 'Bradfield Festival of Music', a revival of a music festival held in the Parish Church on Whit Monday in 1813, 1825 and 1835. During the first two years of the revived Festival the programme was largely comprised of performances by locally based musicians and singers but new ground was broken in 2000 when, for the first time, the Lindsay String Quartet was engaged as the 'headline act'. Following that experience the Festival began to include nationally known artists in its programmes and in 2004 Julian Lloyd Webber, now the Festival's President, performed for the first time at Bradfield.

The Festival now attracts the finest artists from all over the world who perform a wide range of music genres within the classical tradition; last year an ensemble from the world-famous Amsterdam Royal Concertgebouw

Orchestra made the trip up the valley, as did jazz celebrities Jacqui Dankworth and Charlie Wood. At the beginning of this year the organisers announced the programme for 2020: "We are thrilled to welcome back the ensemble from the world-famous Academy of St Martin in the Fields," but of course it never happened. Let's hope that next year we will be able to welcome world-class musicians and singers back up the valley.

Cakin'neet

The singing of locally composed carols is not the only curious tradition that is uniquely celebrated in the valley as the winter nights draw in. When we were children the onset of darker nights towards November would herald the start of the seasonal rounds of cadging cash from unsuspecting neighbours by going 'penny for the Guying' and, in December, carol singing door to door. In this way we earned enough to buy a few fireworks for November 5th and to buy something for mum for Christmas. In Stannington and the villages in the valley the children maintained a more elaborate tradition.

One local, recalling his childhood, recounts that: *"As a kid in the late 60s early 70s we didn't have Halloween or Trick or Treat. Our village had Cakin' Neet. It was a very old tradition celebrated on November 1st where the children in the village used to go around dressed up to houses. The kids would sing the cakin' song and then the householder would give them a bit of cake".*

This song went as follows:

Cake, copper, copper, cake, copper, copper,
If you haven't got a penny, a half penny will do,
If you haven't got half penny,
Then God Bless you.

The significance of this tradition is that it occurred on November 1st, All Souls' Day, when in earlier times it was customary for children to go 'Souling' in many parts of the country. They would go door-to-door begging for pastries with crosses on them called soul-cakes. Sometimes they were given fruit or coins instead. Just like Halloween and The Day of the Dead, symbolically these were treats put out for the dead to appease their souls when they came back to earth for a day. The celebration of Halloween on October 31st is a custom that has only arisen in more recent years but has virtually overtaken the celebration of 'Cakin Neet'.

In its final stages the custom appeared in a new form, oddly, as an adult custom, the converse of most other customs. By the early 1970s it appears to have switched to just a fancy-dress competition focused around three local pubs; The Robin Hood Inn at Little Matlock, The Fox and Glove in Stannington and The Royal in Dungworth. It consisted of local adults, heavily disguised in costume, standing or moving around the bar in silence so that their voices didn't give their identity away. Competitors concealed their identity by wearing a mask or fancy dress, which by tradition had to be of local significance. Having paraded silently from lounge to public bar and back again the competitors went upstairs to be judged. There are rather unsettling photographs of this event taken in 1974 at the Royal Hotel by the celebrated Canadian photographer, Homer Sykes.

6

Along the River

These rivers are very profitable unto ye Lorde in regard of the mills and Cutler Wheels that are turned by theire streames, which wheeles are inployed for the grinding of knives by four or five hundred master workmen.

JOHN HARRISON, SURVEY OF THE MANOR OF SHEFFIELD, 1637.

For centuries the energy of the Loxley was harnessed by the dams, goits, shuttles and weirs that still braid its course and, although the hey-day of water power on the Loxley was between 1750 and 1850, there are enough survivals along the riverside path between Malin Bridge and Damflask to delight the heart of any industrial archaeologist. The earliest mills on the river were corn mills dating from medieval times. The corn mill at Low Bradfield must have been one of the first, being mentioned in a grant to Worksop Abbey by Gerard de Furnival, the lord of the manor, in the thirteenth century. Having been rebuilt many times, it functioned until it burned down during the last war. It's now the delightful spot where families feed the ducks and have picnics in the summer. A second corn mill that stood in the hamlet of Damflask was swept away by the flood of 1864.

It was the development of the use of water power by cutlers as early as the sixteenth century, however, that effectively industrialised the valley. The harnessing of the energy of the river set in motion a major local industry long before the steam-powered industrial revolution of the nineteenth century was to transform the national economy. Records of the building of early cutlers wheels are rare but an early account of a mill called 'Ashton Carr Wheel', about half way along the footpath between Malin Bridge and Damflask, in which William Shooter and Thomas Creswick built a weir and two waterwheels *"with troughs, cogs and trundles"* is dated 1549, in mid Tudor days. By 1700 five of these early cutler's wheels were in use along this stretch of the river and by the end of the century there were at least sixteen. So intensive was the concentration of these mills that in one place along the course of the river a set of three-wheel sites, the Green Wheel, the Glass Tilt and Harrison's Tilt, were built at different levels one above the other along the hillside, all fed by water from the same feeder goit. The same water that had fallen on the far western moors was used over and over again as it tumbled over successive waterwheels. These early industrialists could teach us a thing or two about sustainable energy!

These metal-working mills along Sheffield's rivers fall into three basic categories; forges, where steel ingots were laboriously shaped under heavy tilt hammers; rolling mills, in which red hot steel was drawn into thinner and thinner lengths between stone, or later steel, rollers; and grinding hulls, or 'wheels' which, in its local sense, referred to the mill in which edge tools were ground. All these types of water-powered mills, as well as wire drawing mills, corn mills and paper mills, operated on the Loxley, often changing use with new tenants. Until the early nineteenth century all the metal-working wheels on the Loxley were cutler wheels but, in contrast to the Rivelin valley, where virtually all the mills continued as grinding hulls, there was a gradual shift towards the mills being used for processes of the heavier steel industry with the building of water-powered forges and rolling mills, particularly lower down the valley towards Malin Bridge at Wisewood.

The 'wheels', or 'grinding hulls', were low and barn like, almost agricultural in nature, the term 'hull' being a Yorkshire dialect term for a cow shed, reflecting the dual occupation of the workers. There is no other building that so characterises the Sheffield area. The size of these grinding hulls was accounted in 'troughs', locally pronounced 'trows', the stone troughs that held the water in which the grindstones revolved in order to keep them cool and keep down the dust. Working as outworkers for one of the 'Mesters' in Sheffield, most of the men who earned their living at these wheels were self-employed grinders; reliant on the seasonal flow of water and the cycle of trade. It was an arduous and hazardous way to make a precarious living, each man sitting hunched over a grindstone, cut from the fine local sandstone in a nearby quarry, revolving in a stone trough of water to keep it cool. They would manipulate a 'blank', a rough shaped blade that had been forged in one of the workshops in the valley, against the surface of the grindstone to shape it and give it a cutting edge. It's no wonder that we talk about 'grinding hardships' and keeping 'a nose to the grindstone!' These grinders were men with a reputation for hard drinking and coarse ways but the work they did required incredible skill. They were the custodians of the knowledge of metal and its working that was the foundation of Sheffield's prosperity. During the nineteenth century the millions of table knives, pocket knives and razors that bore the marks of famous Sheffield factories that were held in such high esteem throughout the Empire originated in workshops like these. Rather than letting this heritage simply fall into greater obscurity these valleys should be nominated for World Heritage Site status.

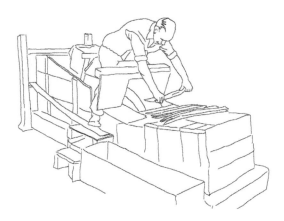

Along the Loxley it is the mill dams and their feeder channels, called goits, and the weirs built into the river to direct the flow, that indicate the position of former mills, although in a few places mill buildings and waterwheels themselves survive, having found new uses. It is testament to the importance of water power here that it continued to be significant so late into the steam age, and, despite every mill bar one having been completely demolished in the 'Great Flood' of 1864, they were all rebuilt in the subsequent twenty years. One or two were actually still using water power into the 1950s. Regrettably, of the many that stood on Sheffield's rivers into the twentieth century, only one now survives complete with its wheels and workings. This is the wheel on the Porter, now a working museum, called Shepherd's Wheel, dating from the mid-seventeenth century.

A recent report by Percival Turnbull for the Don Catchment Rivers Trust in 2012 recognised the unique significance of these sites:

> The importance of Hallamshire to the development of the ferrous metals industry, and in particular of the cutlery trade, is difficult to overstate: by the Middle Ages the name of Sheffield was already synonymous with cutlery, and by the eighteenth century Sheffield was supplying to the world every type of edged tool and weapon. Given this context, the Wheels of the Loxley Valley must be seen to be of far more than local or regional significance: their importance is European, if not more widely international.

May 29th 2020, Malin Bridge

I'm following the four kilometres of footpaths between Malin Bridge and Damflask along the valley bottom, much of it beside the river, and it's easy to access the start of this trail because the Sheffield Supertram route terminates at Malin Bridge. The roads at Malin Bridge are always busy for the core of the old village that was swept away by the flood in 1864 is today little more than a one-way triangular island around which traffic constantly flows from the five roads that converge here.

Just below the spot where the Rivelin and the Loxley meet at Malin Bridge, opposite the Supertram terminus, stands a rather scruffy complex of two storey red-brick industrial buildings, hemmed in between the river and the road, with the name 'La Plata Works' picked out in the brickwork. It's a name that provides a clue to the worldwide market for which this manufacturer of agricultural tools produces. Since 1873 this site, formerly a water-powered mill called the Turner Wheel, has been the premises of Burgon and Ball, known primarily as sheep shear makers. The company was founded almost a 150 years earlier, way back in 1730, but their stock in trade, the production of solid steel sheep shears from the best cast steel rather than the more usual iron of the time, was developed and patented in 1865 by a local cutler called James Ball. So successful were they that annual production of these shears eventually topped 300,000 pairs. Between 1903 and 1906 the firm dabbled, like a number of Sheffield companies, in building early automobiles, their models being named 'La Plata'.

By the 1920s the product range of traditional edge tools had expanded and the firm were producing a huge range of designs of agricultural and garden implements and in the last thirty or forty years, whilst the vast majority of their competitors in Sheffield have folded, the management of Burgon and Ball have managed to steer through the difficult times and adapt to changing demand. In 1974 a new forge and despatch warehouse were built to allow more modern production systems and in 2010 the company established a collaboration with designer Sophie Conran to create award-winning giftware ranges and stainless tools which are now officially endorsed by the Royal Horticultural Society and are featured at Chelsea. In January 2018 the company was bought by Venanpri Tools of Ontario, Canada. One of their representatives commented:

I have carried out technical visits to a huge range of commercial buildings, across the UK and Europe, but the survey of the Burgon & Ball factory, the former water and steam powered facilities with the patina of over almost 300 years of working steel, was rather special. During my two days of inspections I witnessed handcrafted sheep shears being expertly produced in the same way and to the same design as they were back in 1720

-which might not be entirely true but Burgon and Ball is now the name that upholds the tradition of edge tool production in the valley and is recognised worldwide for garden tools and products.

It's not only the remarkable success of the firm, contrasting with the story of hundreds of similar Sheffield enterprises that have gone to the wall, which renders it a curiosity. This factory was featured in the *Guinness Book of Records* in 2000 as being home to the smallest trade union in the world with only ten members! The union, which was established in 1890, was originally known as the 'Sheffield Shear Makers, Grinders, Finishers and Benders Union'. In 1920 it adopted a somewhat more catchy name of the 'Wool Shear Workers Trade Union' with their total membership employed by Burgon and Ball. In 1948 the union held its one and only strike which lasted for two days and accomplished its aim of attaining increased holidays with pay. In 1973 Jim Ballard, the Secretary of the union, who had worked for the firm for 37 years having followed the same path as his father and grandfather, told the *Sheffield Star* newspaper that the subscriptions hadn't been increased since the union was founded in 1890. In 1997 they proudly issued a statement after the 1997 general election that 100% of their membership had voted Labour. In 2007 however, the union ceased to exist and the baton for the smallest union in the TUC passed to the 'Card Setting Machine Tenters Society', who have a whopping eighty-eight members.

Wisewood

Passing La Plata works I take my life in my hands and cross Stannington Road to look over the bridge parapet at the waterwheel that powered the Malin Bridge Corn Mill. It's an undershot wheel at the end of a short leat from the river, turned directly by the flow passing beneath it. It's the only undershot wheel in the valley as this arrangement could not supply enough energy to power metal working mills and forges. The wheel is in good repair, though it no longer turns, and the stone-built mill has survived in a number of guises. In the '90s it became an American Diner for a while but now it's been resurrected as 'Corn Mill Court' residences.

From Malin Bridge it's only a short walk up Loxley Road before the signpost points down to the start of the footpath that slants through the trees towards the river. I've followed this path many, many times over the years and I never fail to discover something new. Here the traffic noise dies away, replaced by birdsong and the gentle sounds of the river. The footpath traces a unique riparian landscape of former industry, thickly wooded, completely hidden and unsuspected until you get amongst it. It's a landscape that has a dual personality, at the same time urban and rural, an area defined by Richard Mabey and other recent writers as 'Edgeland', part of the semi-urban, forgotten fringe that surrounds most towns and cities. To the left of the path the river, that here is curiously stained a sickly bright orange colour by the emissions from former mine workings somewhere further along the bank, is screened by ugly graffitied concrete slabs and along the right-hand side runs a tall, rusting wire-mesh fence enclosing a mysterious, impenetrable scrub of willows and tall reeds. Decaying notices warn of the danger of trespassing due to deep water. This is the site of the silted dam of Wisewood Rolling Mill. Photographs of this area in the early twentieth century depict scenes of heavy industry; tall belching chimneys and gaunt brick sheds. Today no signs remain of these former forge and mill buildings, although massive stone blocks mark the overflow from the dam.

A little further on the mesh fencing is replaced by a neatly clipped hedge and the marshy wasteland becomes the manicured lawns of 'Loxley Village', a recently built complex of retirement apartments, the building of which was fiercely contested back in 2006 by the Loxley Valley Preservation Society. The buildings seem to me well designed and the layout very attractive, two of the blocks actually mirror the design of the former Wisewood Forge that stood on this site and it's no surprise that the development has won awards for the architects DWA Architects Ltd. To me this development stands as a shining example of how 'Edgeland' can be restored and recovered sensitively.

Although there are now the remains of only two Wisewood mills there are records that there were at least four scythe grinding wheels on this lower part of the river from the early sixteenth century. A rental agreement of 1777 shows that here at the 'Upper Mill', now occupied by the Loxley Village Retirement

Home complex, stood two hulls, each with thirteen-foot diameter overshot wheels powering twenty-eight 'troughs' employing thirty men. By the early nineteenth century the mill had been rebuilt as a tilt forge and rolling mill. When W. T. Miller carried out his exhaustive survey of Sheffield watermills, which was published in the 1930s as *The Watermills of Sheffield*, two of the mills at Wisewood were still in use, the wheels having been replaced by turbines to power the tilt hammers and the rolling mill. Between those dates the mills had undergone a complete and total destruction following the collapse of the embankment of the Dale Dyke reservoir on the night of March 11th 1864.

It is somewhat ironic that the Dale Dyke Dam further up the valley, whose embankment failed so spectacularly in 1864, had been built to impound water that would compensate the mill owners for the loss of flow caused by the building of the other three dams, for its collapse released a torrent that destroyed every mill but one in its destructive path down the valley. Samuel Harrison, in his '*Complete History of the Great Flood at Sheffield*', graphically recorded the scenes of the aftermath. Here at the upper Wisewood works he recounts;

> The water wheel and ponderous machinery is laid bare and massive iron castings scattered about the in the vicinity. The scene here is one that excites wonder. It can hardly be believed that such masses of metal and of rock could have been tossed about like playthings buy the force of the water.

And of the lower works he says;

> Wisewood Works have been swept away completely, except that an immense water, fly and other wheels are to be seen in the ground half covered with the mud and the debris of the flood, looking as singular and out of place as the Sphynx partially submerged beneath the sands of Egypt. Near the works is a large stone that has attracts much notice. It is of immense size, and is supposed to weigh about twenty tons.

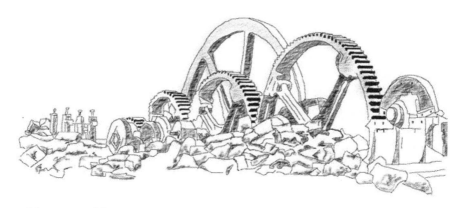

The ruins of the Wisewood mills, so vividly described by Harrison, attracted the particular attention of visitors to the aftermath of the flood. The scene of the smashed machinery sticking out of the scoured bed of the river is one of the many iconic images of the event that were recorded by early photographers. Ladies in their crinolines and gents in tall top hats standing beside the wheels make it a particularly poignant and improbable image. These photographs depict a devastated landscape so different from today's wooded valley that it's difficult to imagine either how it could have recovered so completely during the intervening years or how the mill owners could have rebuilt so quickly. Most of the rebuilding costs were funded by compensation payments made by the Water Company to the mill owners, in this case £8,750.

An enigmatic sculpture, a huge iron shape, originally one of the bases for the giant forge hammers of Wisewood Forge, stands beside the path overlooking the tranquil scene of the well-maintained mill dam that stretches away beside the path beyond the retirement home. Alders and graceful willows line the bank, their branches sweeping across the water. The water looks fresh and clear, and it's a popular fishing spot, used by the South Yorkshire Police Angling Club, where roach, perch, bream, pike and the occasional chub thrive. There's a sudden commotion as a pugnacious coot, wings stretched and beak open, pursues a group of mallards across the lake, protecting his mate and her three chicks. The footpath continues along an embankment between the dam and the river, which runs some fifteen feet below the level of the water in the dam. Built into the wall beside the river the rounded edge of a huge grindstone, six feet in diameter, protrudes. Long since reused as building material, it would once have been used in one of the nearby mills to grind scythe blades.

As I continue along the path beside the dam the birdsong becomes drowned by the river as it roars down a substantially-built stone weir, built to direct the flow of the river into the dam. On the opposite bank stands a very recently erected brick building. The enterprising landowner is using the same weir to direct the water onto a turbine in the form of an Archimedes screw that extends from the building down to the river. I later discover that a firm called 'Wisewood Hydro', was responsible for developing the project in 2017, estimating that the turbine will generate the equivalent power to the electrical consumption of twelve average households, saving about 45 tonnes of CO_2 per year from coal-fired power stations. It's mesmerising to watch the huge green screw turn, accompanied by a regular slap, slapping, churning sound that is so reminiscent of the old waterwheels. Let's hope that this is successful and is the precursor to many such schemes along Sheffield's rivers.

Around the next bend I'm stopped in my tracks by a scene reminiscent of archaeological excavations of an ancient Greek or Roman site. The ground is pitted with heaps and hollows, and on both sides of the path lie, seemingly at random, huge blocks of cut stone, rectangular, obelisk like, tumbled cuboids, each of which must weigh tons, and colossal old wooden beams. The remains of a wall of similar blocks is built into the bank, and more blocks are arranged on top. To the right, on the opposite side of the path, a silted dam has been colonised by prehistoric-looking ferns and horsetails; nature reclaiming her own. Despite this footpath being designated 'The Loxley Valley Trail' there's no interpretation board and nothing to tell the many walkers that follow it what these remarkable remains relate to. It's only by examining the old maps of the area that it becomes apparent that here we have the remains of the 'Loxley Valley Steelworks', built in 1868 on the site of the Broadhead Wheel that had been destroyed in the flood. The massive stonework is the surviving back wall against which two huge wheels, sixteen feet in diameter by eight feet wide, turned in their wheel pits, powering the hammers that forged steel for armaments in the First World War. Miller says that *"During and after the War these premises were greatly extended and water power became entirely inadequate. Now they are completely dismantled and hardly the shell of a building remains."* The site is certainly one of the most poignant reminders of the era of water powered industry along any of Sheffield's rivers.

A short distance further along stand a group of buildings terraced above one another on the hillside. Remarkably, so intensive was the use of water power, that here there were three mills, the Green Wheel, the Glass Tilt and

Harrison's Tilt and Forge, that were all fed from the same long leat, the water falling down from the tail race of one wheel to turn the next. The Green Wheel, being the uppermost, was the only mill in the valley to escape the flood's destructive force. The mill buildings themselves no longer exist but a set of gates open into a wide yard, at one side of which stands a charming nineteenth-century stone cottage, presumably the manager's house, facing onto a long, narrow dam at which a man sits quietly fishing. In the next yard stands a stone built, barn-like building; the surviving building of the Glass Tilt, surrounded by wrecked cars and, most curiously, an old fire engine from Llandudno! How the mill became called the Glass Tilt is not recorded but it's unlikely to have ever had anything to do with glass. I'd love to look inside to see if any workings survive but the place is deserted and there's an unwelcoming air of dilapidation, reinforced by warning signs to 'Keep out, guard dogs'. I take the hint.

According to Samuel Harrison just below this stood a further wheel known as Harrison's Forge which, he tells us, felt the full impact and was swept away, together with the bodies of twenty-year-old Joseph Gregory and sixteen-year-old Walter Booth. *"They were working all night as usual,"* he recounts, *"no one saw or heard them at the time they perished."* Booth's body was found half a mile below but that of Gregory was either never discovered or it was one of the dozens that were buried without having been identified, a terrible indictment of the working conditions of the Victorian era.

May 22nd 2020, Little Matlock.

A few hundred yards beyond the Glass Tilt stands a group of buildings known as 'Little Matlock'. The original forge of 1732, which originally stood beside the river here, was completely destroyed by the flood in 1864 but the building that replaced it has the date 1882 on the gable wall; it's Little Matlock Rolling

Mill and I've come to pay homage to its 18 foot 6 inch diameter overshot water wheel, the largest surviving in the Sheffield area.

But I'm in for a shock. The last time that I saw the massive iron wheel a walkway had been constructed alongside the tail goit to give access to view it but today the whole thing is completely overgrown with scrub and brambles and inaccessible. At first I think that the wheel itself has gone but it's just about possible to make out the outline of the buckets behind the tangle of enveloping growth. It's deeply disappointing to discover yet again the little regard in which the unique industrial heritage of Sheffield is held but I really should have got used to it by now.

"At the bottom of the valley, near the bed of the river, were the tilts and forges of Messrs. Chapman and Mrs. Denton and also a row of strongly built and good looking stone houses inhabited by the Chapmans," wrote Samuel Harrison, but the mill buildings, wheels and cottages that stood here were all swept away in 1864. It's difficult to imagine the horror of what occurred on the night of the flood when the water punched a hole through the home of Daniel Chapman, washing him and six other members of his family to their deaths. Next door lived Daniel's brother Thomas, with his wife, four children and their servant girl. Thomas had the horrific experience of witnessing his son being swept out of the window and carried down the river in the brown, foaming torrent.

The mill was rebuilt as a rolling mill driven by the overshot water wheel. Remarkably, the mill remained water driven until 1956, when it was converted to electricity under the ownership of Kenyon Brothers and Co, Ltd. The water wheel has since remained immobile, off its bearings, covered in vegetation and in need of renovation. Above the wheel is a huge cast iron pentrough. In the 1950s it was estimated that the wheel could generate twenty-five horse power, enough to drive a sixteen ton flywheel that provided the enormous torque required to drive the rolls through which the steel ingots were fed. The floor throughout is covered in heat-resisting, fireproof, steel plates which allowed hot metal to be moved around easily.

In 1974 the plant was sold to a company called Barworth Flockton Ltd. and in the mid-1980s I was fortunate to have visited the mill and watched in fascination as the team of rollers dextrously manhandled red hot steel ingots, that had been heated in the furnace at the back of the building, backwards and forwards between the two-high rollers. As in most operations in the steel industry this was incredibly skilled work, each man on the team entirely reliant on each other to ensure their safety, as the steel became ever thinner and longer, passing quickly backwards and forwards through the rolls and back over the top, until it became a thin, lithe, red hot snake shooting from the rolls and coiling across the floor.

In 1997 the company was taken over but shortly ceased to operate. The site was sold to a development company who planned to convert the former mill into a residential housing. Thanks to the historical importance of the site, however, Sheffield City Council stepped in and prevented the transaction, and in 2001 a company called Pro-Roll Ltd. bought the mill buildings and revived traditional hand-rolling, producing specialist steel bars for the aerospace, oilfield engineering, bio-medical implants, defence, architectural, construction, electronics, and marine industries and counted Rolls Royce, Ferrari and Corus among its many prestigious customers. Its speciality was the production of low volumes of high-grade section in special alloys and materials such as titanium. But it wasn't all plain sailing producing such high spec products in such historic buildings. The Grade 2 listing included much of the company's equipment which posed problems from time to time when spares were no longer available. In 2017 the company relocated to a new site at Pluto Works, Penistone Road, where it has been able to expand production as one of the very few still able to hand roll steel and alloys. The mill buildings at Little Matlock, however, have been unoccupied and the gates locked ever since.

There's an attractive wooden footbridge just behind the mill that looks as though it was designed especially for playing Poohsticks. The river here is wide and tree shaded and I cross into the deep shade of huge beeches and oaks. This side of the river is deeply wooded and bright sunlight shafts through the tissue-paper fresh foliage. A blackcap and a chiffchaff, blackbird and wren join in chorus. There are wide paths through the woodland, stone edged, with the remains of little wooden bridges crossing tiny brooks, rather like a long-forgotten park. The valley is narrow and steep sided and it's a steep climb up a cobbled footpath through the wood, aided by the handrail that gives welcome protection from the hundred-foot sheer drop down to the river. I'm quite out of breath as I approach an imposing three storey stone-built building that stands at the top on the edge of the wood. The features are Georgian with no-nonsense symmetrical rectangular windows and a central doorway facing down towards the river. A curious stone inscription in Latin above the doorway reads:

Nec vos dulcisime mundi
Nomina, Vos Montes, cataractae, Pescus, Syvae
Rupes atque Caverae, anima raments reliquas.

Thomas Halliday 1804

It all relates to a somewhat unfortunate speculative venture by the Reverend Thomas Halliday, the eccentric Unitarian minister of Norton on the other side of Sheffield who, you will remember, had purchased an allotment of fifty acres of Wadsley Moor on the opposite side of the valley and built a house there, which he called Loxley House. Whilst living there he became struck by the beauty of this spot along River Loxley, then known as Cliff Rocher, considering it comparable to Matlock in Derbyshire. Using his wife's money he began a remarkable project, setting about the transformation of this steep wooded hillside into what he called 'Little Matlock', the name it retains to this day. Steps and walks, signs of which remain, were cut into the rocky hillside and trees and shrubs were planted in order to accentuate the similarity to the picturesque valley in Derbyshire. The massive beech trees probably date from this planting. Halliday's enterprise did not stop there, however. At the top of the steep wooded incline he built the house, one half of which was used as a refreshment house, initially known as 'The Rock Inn' and later renamed 'The Robin Hood & Little John'. Still grieving for a relative that had died in a house fire, Halliday was determined that the same eventuality could not befall this house so it was built almost entirely from stone, including the staircases, as a 'fireproof house'. The area was opened to the public and for some years apparently attracted large numbers of visitors from Sheffield during the summer months. Samuel Harrison gives an eloquent description of the spot as he found it in 1864:

We now reach Little Matlock, one of the most romantic and picturesque scenes in the neighbourhood of Sheffield, a place to which, it is said, Robin Hood and Little John used frequently to resort. The grounds of Little Matlock and the Rock Inn lie above, on the precipitous and finely wooded declivity of a steep hill, which in summer attracts thousands of visitors to enjoy the sequestered walks, to ramble amongst the rocks, or to descend into the beautiful valley where the river Loxley ripples and foams along in its rocky and shady bed.

It is extremely difficult to imagine the ladies and gentlemen in costumes of the Jane Austen era promenading through the woodland walks and struggling up the hill to the refreshment rooms, even though the flowery Latin inscription that still stands above the door entices them with an evocation of the lovely surroundings; the mountains, cataracts, pastures, woods, rocks and caves which Halliday says he never wishes to leave. Unfortunately, however, he had overstretched himself financially and poverty did indeed force him to move the family away.

The building survived as a pub however. The most celebrated of the many families that kept the house over the years was the Furness family who had it for nearly seventy years from 1886 until 1952. Matthew Furness, until quite late in life, managed to combine dual occupations in the traditional local manner by being the licensee of the Robin Hood as well as a coal and gannister miner. His one-man operated mine was at the foot of the slope and a small Morris engine was installed at the top to haul laden trucks up the incline.

On a piece of rough ground on the hillside a little beyond the Robin Hood can be picked out the remains of a rifle range; a brick-built butt on the side of the hill and a trench into which the targets could be lowered for changing. The Sheffield & District Rifle Club used the Robin Hood Inn as its headquarters until 1960 when, it has been said, a serious accident occurred in which a walker was shot! The Laing family ran the pub for about thirty years from the 1970s and in 2003 it was purchased by the Appleyards and, completely renovated, it was run by daughter Keeley. The Robin Hood enjoyed a brief golden era, at one stage attaining the 'Visit England Silver Award' but it was remote. Situated here at the end of a very long, narrow lane from the lower valley, it was probably the most difficult pub to reach in Sheffield! This, and difficult trading conditions, contributed to its final and very sad closure in 2011. It has been renovated as three private cottages and retains the features much as it was built.

Back along the riverside footpath there's a row of red brick workers houses called Olive Terrace before I come to the Olive Wheel itself, where the mill building, originally a paper mill, has recently been redeveloped for residential use. After the flood the banks of the river for miles below were strewn with paper that had been washed out of the mill. The twin waterwheels still survive, but they are hidden beneath the mill building and out of sight. On the opposite bank of the dam that stretches beyond the buildings stands an attractive house, its gardens stretching to the waters' edge. At the time of the flood it belonged to the mill owner, Mr Woodward, whose conservatories were flooded and his plants damaged.

October 1st 2020, Stoneface, Storrs Brook

The path soon reaches Rowel Bridge, the only road crossing between Loxley and Stannington on this stretch of the river. I look over the bridge parapet and see water pouring through a large wooden box, called a pentrough, which originally directed and controlled the flow of water onto a wheel. There are no remains of the 1734 mill itself where, in 1794, forty men were employed and I pause for a moment to consider the fate of William Bradbury, a grinder who, we are told in Samuel Harrison's book, *"being anxious to make a good wage on Saturday night, had stopped behind his companions and was working all night."* Imagine that. An enormous level of skill and dexterity was required to fine grind the shape into blank knife blades by manipulating them against a revolving stone at the best of times but the idea of continuing the operation into this cold, dark night by the light of flickering candles is quite inconceivable. *"No one saw what became of Bradbury but he has not been seen or heard of since,"* continues Harrison, *"and there is no doubt he was carried away by the flood. His body has not been recovered; at least it has not been identified."*

Beside Rowell Bridge the Storrs Brook tumbles through the woods to join the river, and the road beside it follows the bottom of the deep, rather gloomy, wooded valley. Beyond a short terrace of six sunless workers cottages beside the stream stands a most curious and beautiful stretch of drystone wall enclosing nothing. The stones have been laid in a swirling pattern and seem to flow around two stone roundels on which words like 'engulfed', 'thunderous' and 'deluge' spiral into the centre like a whirlpool. The wall is effectively a piece of sculpture commemorating the flood and it stands as a gateway to a remarkable project. Beyond this piece of walling the bottom of Beacon Wood, through which the stream flows, has been transformed into a woodland gallery with curiously-shaped sculptures of different materials beside a meandering footpath. The pieces are sheer fantasy, mythical, mysterious, clearly the product of an imaginative mind. Here's the naked, curled figure of a woman in stone, sheltered by the roots of an enormous beech tree; there's a huge stone head in the ferns, one eye awake and the other asleep; here's a rearing horse constructed from scaffolding poles and there's a sparkling iridescent silver figure running through the wood, constructed from old CDs; here's a great blank face, beautifully carved from stone, surrounded by leafy branches that reminds me of the green man in Bradfield church.

A sign pinned to a tree says 'Stoneface Creative.' This is all the work of one man, the remarkable Andrew Vickers. He likes to tell the story that, having discovered a love and a talent for carving, he outgrew his workshop. As a local child he had played in Storrs Wood and had an idea that it would make the perfect place to work but couldn't imagine how this could come about. One day, happening to bump into the lady who owned the woodland in a local shop, without any real hope, he asked if she would like to sell it. Remarkably she agreed and he's now well established, having landscaped the space with a pond, a bridge and footpaths that wind between the majestic beech trees, his sculptures positioned along it so that they can be viewed from the road. As well as taking commissions he organises woodland events here and it suddenly strikes me that here we have the successor to Thomas Halliday's project at Little Matlock a few hundred yards down the river.

In 2017 Sheffield's Lord Mayor, Graham Oxley launched an appeal to raise money for a memorial for local members of the Armed Forces who have fallen in various wars and campaigns since the end of the Second World War. He attained the support of the Royal British Legion, Sir Nick Clegg and Lord David Blunkett and approached Andrew Vickers with the commission to create a memorial that did not glorify war and that could be a gathering point for people of any religion or none. The result is an extraordinary paved area which stands beside the road where two very moving and arresting stone figures of women in mourning sit on a low wall. One, heavily draped, her long hair falling free, sits downcast in grief whilst the other, looks up through the trees to the sky, in hope. It's a moving monument in a beautiful setting.

From beside the flood memorial wall I climb the long, steep flight of steps that lead into Beacon Wood. A sign beside the path indicates that the wood belongs to the Woodland Trust, purchased from a private owner in 1989. It's part of a wide band of ancient oak woodland that cloaks the steep southern side of this section of the valley. The wood is alive with spring birdsong and the scent from the deep blue carpet of bluebells is intoxicating. Patches of wood sorrel, wood anemone and yellow archangel appear beside the path, strong indicator species typical of ancient woodland, and historical records show that the wood was in existence here 400 years ago, defining it as 'ancient'. In 1841 the wood was known as Baeon Wood a name derived from a previous owner, Mr Richard Baeon who purchased some land in 1604 in the area around Worth House between Dungworth and Storrs.

Like most of the ancient woodlands around Sheffield the wood is full of dips and hollows, the heritage of old coal and gannister workings. Beacon Wood, in addition, displays remains of sunken air-raid shelters which served the local brick factory during the Second World War when it was commissioned for the production of ordnance. Timber that was removed in 1998 as part of the woodland management proved worthless to the contractor and had to be disposed of as it was full of bomb shrapnel! It was not even suitable to be used for firewood due to the danger of hitting metal fragments when cutting it.

The path leads down to the right back towards the river and emerges behind a terrace of six brick-built worker's houses that face a wide expanse of garages and workshops of a company that restores vintage cars. A metal bridge at the other side of the wide yard crosses the river. But here I am met with a scene of hideous industrial dereliction, shockingly out of place in this picturesque valley. Beside the path, amongst piles of burned rubbish, rusting wire and dumped building materials, stands a rusting collection of shipping containers, one labelled 'China Shipping'. Derelict, asbestos-clad factory buildings, vandalised, graffitied and dangerous, stretch along the riverside, fenced off by miles of damaged grey-mesh fencing. These are the abandoned remains of Storrs Fire Clay Works, owned until 1992 by a company called Thomas Marshall's who produced refractory materials for the steel industry from fire clay originally mined in the hillside opposite.

Marshall's Brick Works

When I first followed this path in the 1970s production was still in full swing, refractory bricks being fired in domed kilns beside the river. Today it's a dystopian landscape, grey and gaunt, reminiscent of scenes from the old Soviet Union. There are those evidently for whom such landscapes hold a fascination, and any number of internet blogs with names like 'Oblivion' and 'Nightcrawler' display photos of this site featuring tumbled tunnels, flooded factory buildings, mangled machinery and sawn-off padlocks. Other people, like folk singer and musician Jon Boden, who lives nearby, find reassurance from the way that nature is reclaiming the abandoned factory where, from every crack in the concrete, birch trees and brambles sprout and lurid-coloured mosses seem to be eating away at the edges. His recent album *Songs from the Floodplain* takes its inspiration partly from these skeletal structures and relics that echo to the ghosts of past workers.

The presence of these cheerless remains can be traced back to the fact that certain clays outcrop along the sides of the valley, in thin layers between the seams of gritstone and coal, of the carboniferous rock sequence. These materials are known as pot clay, or fire-clay, and gannister (it appears that the word can be spelled with one 'n' or two). These seams occur at the base of the thin layers of coal and are the remains of the earth in which the coal-forming forests grew 280 million years ago. True gannister is a hard flint-like rock with a very high silica content of over 90% whilst pot clay is softer and can be moulded. It's doubtful if many people have even heard of gannister but it played a vital part in the early development of the steel industry. By the mid-seventeenth century the unique properties of these materials, in being able to withstand very high temperatures, were being already being exploited to produce crucibles and furnace linings for the glass industry in the nearby Ewden Valley at Bolsterstone, but the local industry of mining the materials and manufacturing fire bricks in the Loxley Valley began with the birth of the Sheffield steel industry, when Benjamin Huntsman in the 1740s first developed the technique of casting steel in crucible pots. In fact it is probable that Doncaster-born Huntsman was drawn to Sheffield by the local availability of the clays with which to make the crucibles that could withstand the temperature of 600 degrees Centigrade needed to melt steel, as well as to make refractory bricks with which to line the specially designed furnaces. Following many experiments and failures he was finally successful in his Handsworth workshop, and the Sheffield steel industry was born!

During the nineteenth century the demand for steel and therefore for gannister and pot clay rose and rose with new techniques of steel melting. Bessemer converters, blast furnaces and steel ladles all required lining with gannister fire bricks and mining the thin seams in the Loxley Valley became an industry in itself. Most of the mines were small scale drift mines drilled into the hillsides and operated by a few men although on Loxley and Wadsley Common operations were on a larger scale and much of that area is riddled with abandoned tunnels and workings. At its peak this local industry was of such a scale that it gave employment to around a thousand men.

Nearby, at the head of Load Brook, there remains a small cluster of buildings that developed from a lonely moorland farm to a minor industrial site in the late nineteenth and early twentieth centuries after a 'pot clay' mine was developed by William Trickett, a local farmer who obtained rights to mine pot clay from the landowner, the Duke of Norfolk in 1852. William Trickett died in 1890 and the business was continued by his three sons, William, Benjamin and Matthew. The mine was officially named the 'Intake Clay Pit' and had four drift entrances going into the hillside, one of which is still visible. The path of a former tramway, along which ponies would haul the clay wagons from the mine to the brick works, can also still be seen, as can the cottages that were built to house the workers. With a pair of powerful rock crushers and three coal-fired brick kilns with tall, puthering chimneys in operation this was a busy industrial site, difficult to imagine today. The mine was taken over by Thomas Wragg & Sons, and closed as recently as the 1950s. Today the cottages have been restored as attractive holiday accommodation.

Wraggs also owned a pot clay mine and refractory brick works immediately to the south east of Ughill, which, in the early 1970s was producing 15,000 tons of clay a year, at which stage the company optimistically stated, *"The mine can be worked at the present rate for 100 years."* However the Ughill mine had drainage problems and although powerful pumps had been installed in the 1950s to pump between 600 and 800 gallons per minute from the mine, it closed in November 1977. Today the site has been landscaped and no sign remains of this formerly important enterprise.

Mining gannister, as distinct for pot-clay mining, was an unusually hazardous occupation as the dust to which the miners were exposed is nearly pure silica and so they experienced an excessive mortality from phthisis. An entry in the Parliamentary record of Hansard shows that the danger was well appreciated at the highest levels. On 11 April 1910, Mr Steel-Maitland asked how many deaths from pneumoconiosis, bronchitis and other lung diseases, respectively, had occurred each year in the valley of the Don above Sheffield in which gannister mines are situated. His question was answered by none other than Winston Churchill who replied that: *"Since the special rules were established in May 1905, the inspector informs me that there is far less dust, and the ventilation is much better now in these mines, and that workers and officials are agreed that the effect has been most beneficial"* – a somewhat evasive answer implying that It was indeed a most hazardous occupation.

Once mined the raw gannister was crushed to make clay that could be moulded to form any shape required and then fired in rounded brick kilns on the site by the local firms of Thomas Wragg & Sons at Old Wheel Brick Works and Thomas Marshall and Co. at Storrs Bridge Brick Works, which later became Hepworths, and Dysons at the Griffs. As the steel industry declined however, so too did the need for the materials involved in its production and the gannister and pot clay mining industries fell into rapid decline. The production of refractory materials ceased altogether in the area in the 1990s.

On a recent walk I was surprised to discover, behind the fence at the rear of the brand-new houses that have recently been built on the site of Dyson's brick factory on the Griffs hillside, an opening in a low cliff face, about five feet high, closed off with a locked gate. A stream ran from the opening. Peering inside I could see a barrel-vaulted tunnel leading back into the hillside, lined with timber and supported by an arch of spaced iron hoops; the entrance to a disused drift mine and one of the few clues remaining of this former industry that was so important locally.

One of the men who worked in these mines, Mr Jack Goodison, recorded some of his reminiscences to the BBC in 2006:

> I spent most of my working life of nearly 50 years in the clay mines of the Loxley Valley, and that's where I was during the war. In those days, there were three firms in the Loxley Valley, Dysons, Thomas Marshall's and Thomas Wragg and Sons and between them they supplied 95% of all the hollow refractories made in the steel works all over Great Britain. I worked for Thomas Wragg as man and boy in all 7 or 8 pits, including Ughill, at one time or other, in the Stannington Pot Clay Seam. When war was declared, I went and signed up like everyone else. I'd wanted to go in the Navy, but as mining was a reserved occupation, I was told I was going back down the pit! Mining was a very wet job, despite 3 pumps working constantly, and every so often there were floods, which were difficult to bring under control. I was buried three times, so I was always very careful about safety procedures, and went round the men every afternoon without fail to make sure they were OK. Our industry was vital to the war effort, and if the Germans had bombed the Loxley Valley successfully, the war would have been over very quickly.

Marshall's abandoned factory site opposite the Old Wheel dam, following years and years of dereliction, was purchased in 2006 by the house building company, Bovis Homes Group. They intended to redevelop the site and build 500 homes. However, in the face of stiff opposition from the Loxley Valley Protection Society, the Loxley Valley Design Group, the Campaign to Protect Rural England and Bradfield Parish Council, planning permission was refused. In December 2019 development plans were revived, with a new proposal by Parkin Properties to redevelop the site and build 350 new homes on the Marshall's site which is proving as unpopular with local residents as the previous proposal. The 'Friends of the Loxley Valley' group are now studying the plans carefully before submitting a detailed response. *"We initially hoped there would be elements of it that we could support, but so far we can't find any. We will therefore be submitting a very strong objection,"* they have said. Although Patrick Properties say they will create 'a sustainable neighbourhood' the group think the township is far too big, leading to heavy demands on local roads, schools and communities and intrusion of noise and light pollution. *"We worry that this new township could easily become an isolated car-dependent enclave of executive homes,"* says the group. *"We suspect this planning application may be putting private profit before the needs and aspirations of the local community."* The local MP, Olivia Blake, has written to express her full support for these arguments and a local protest campaign has been launched.

It appears most unlikely to me that this overambitious plan will ever get the go ahead but we will await developments. Meanwhile the problem of how to resolve the problem of how to deal with such dangerous and unsightly ruins remains. I see that someone is now proposing that these plans are dropped in favour of building a 'Medieval village celebrating the local links with Robin Hood'. Well, best of luck with that idea.

October 28th 2019. Storrs Bridge Fishing Pond

To the right of the footpath that skirts the industrial wasteland stands the next mill site along the footpath called the 'Old Wheel'. When I first walked this path, although none of the mill buildings survived, there were two rusting waterwheels still embedded in the bank here. Now they are gone. Above the bank the long dam that fed the wheels, however, still stretches out beside the path, home to a company of ducks and geese. The rustic stone buildings of Old Wheel Farm on the other side of the pond are reflected in the water. I once stood here with a party of children to be entertained by a pair of herons squabbling over a large fish. The pond was completely frozen and they slipped and slithered across the ice on their stilt-like legs in a comically ungainly match so much in contrast to their usual stately demeanour.

Beyond the industrial ruins of Marshall's the stretch of footpath is a tree-lined delight. The path leads between the river on one side and the head goit of the Old Wheel dam on the other. Alongside the path stands a large stone with a curious inscription, 'MARK BELOW TWO FEET ABOVE WEIR AS AGREED 1825'. It records the settlement of a dispute over water levels between the two neighbouring mill owners, a regular occurrence when river levels were low. The river here tumbles down a substantial stone weir. A lone heron stands statue still in the middle of the white torrent before unfolding its great wings and floating gracefully away across the fields. The weir directs water, via a sluice opened by a shuttle, into the head goit channel, yet another example of how the whole river environment has been engineered over the centuries to efficiently reuse the same water over and over again.

A flight of ancient worn stone steps leads to Storrs Bridge Lane, at the bottom of which piles of old masonry and tipped rubbish are all that remains of Claremont House; the once proud grand Victorian home of Thomas Marshall, original owner of the refractory nearby. It's a depressing approach to the dam of Storrs Bridge Wheel between yet more decay and dereliction and as I approach the dam, things don't look any more promising. There's a jumble of scruffy, rusting metal sheds with blue peeling paint that look as if they were once shipping containers. The signboard that stands next to them is not particularly welcoming. Below the heading 'Loxley Fisheries' are listed thirteen rules to be observed, one mysteriously prohibiting "boilers, jokers, bloodworm and catmeat." To anglers this is known as 'Marshall's Pond' after the nearby brickworks. Having never caught anything larger than a tiddler in a net this world of the fisherman is alien and a mystery to me.

Through the trees the vista opens onto a tranquil scene. The sky is reflected deep blue in the still water of the triangular lake that during the eighteenth and nineteenth centuries fed three large waterwheels powering the forges, grinding wheels and a rolling mill that stood here. Today only tall alders frame the banks, and spaced between them, well wrapped against the clear, cold morning, sit men on stools in quiet contemplation of rods extending over the water. Following the bank round the lake I try to avoid tripping over bits of tackle and accoutrements, bait boxes, keep nets and the like, that surround each huddled figure. They are so absorbed into their own watery world that I feel somewhat intimidated about disturbing them. However, there are a couple of young lads and I ask how they are doing. *"Not bad, we've had a nine-pound carp this morning,"* replies a tall blond boy called Tom, lifting his arms wide in the age-old manner of angler's tales to signify its size. I must have looked sceptical because he took out his mobile phone to show me a photo that he'd taken of it. Sure enough, there he was proudly holding a very handsome two-foot-long fish with a round open mouth, patterned with scales, bluish above and bronze below. I was duly impressed. I was somewhat incredulous, however, of Tom's story that Kevin, the fisherman next along the bank, had recently landed a sturgeon! This seemed so unlikely that I interrupted Kevin in his reverie. *"Oh yes, I've had him three or four times,"* he said, switching on his pocket camera on which there was indeed a photo of him holding a long thin greenish fish with a suckerish mouth; undeniably a sturgeon. *"The owner must have put him in some time ago."* *"Has he got a name?"* I asked, and, getting a blank reply, immediately regretted it.

A little way along the bank a collection of plastic models catches my eye. On closer inspection they turn out to be sad little memorials to men whose fishing days were passed. A white angel bears the words 'Dave, Always in our Hearts' and 'Grandad, Sadly Missed' inscribed on a heart. Alongside, in the wet grass, is a weather worn photo of a bearded man, presumably Dave, proudly holding a large fish. A couple of pairs of mandarin ducks, flamboyant orientals, have taken up residence on one of the artificial islands that are moored in the middle of the lake.

Today's fishermen may be surprised to learn that fishing the waters in the valley may have a long history, for one explanation of the derivation of the river's name, 'Lox', appears to come from Middle High German as 'lahs' meaning salmon, that became the Old English leax. Lox is a word still used for a Yiddish cured salmon dish. So 'Loxley', if we accept this derivation, is the clearing beside the salmon river. Personally I'm not convinced. (Wikipedia, by the way, has it that 'lox' is derived from 'Lynx', a derivation that is completely without authority elsewhere.) Whatever, it's a long time since salmon swam up the river but, according to the Don Catchment Rivers Trust, the River Loxley and nearby Rivelin provide the best potential for future spawning of salmon in the Don Catchment due to the structure and quality of the river bed and the presence of gravels. The weirs that fragment the river, however, make it inaccessible to most migratory fish, including trout and salmon. Accordingly, the Trust are presently investigating the feasibility of constructing channels to bypass the weirs and improving conditions in the river to give free passage for fish, migratory salmon and trout as well as brook lamprey. There is very good reason to be optimistic about this proposal as, remarkably, the water quality in the formerly filthy Don has improved to such an extent that salmon have indeed returned. The first evidence of them reproducing in the river was found downstream in the River Dearne in 2015. I'm looking forward to the day that they find their way up the Loxley, the river named after them.

7

Lakeland

You may stand on the hillside and watch the men at their various work until you might dream that a settlement of colonists had just arrived in a new country and were building their first city in the most beautiful locality they could find. The steam engine is running about on a tramway; the steady horse drags a number of trucks laden with soil, whilst the men are either working in gangs on the puddle wall or dextrously picking masses from the hillside that needs lowering.

REV. ALFRED GATTY,
SHEFFIELD, PAST AND PRESENT (1873)

June 30th 2020, Damflask

I've now reached Stacey Bank and it's as far as we can follow the riverside walk. Beyond this point the river flows through a manmade landscape of a different sort. For the next eight kilometres the valley floor is braided by four massive reservoirs. The first has inherited the name of the little village that it drowned, Damflask, and it's popular with fishermen, walkers and sailors.

The five kilometre circuit of Damflask Reservoir is the most popular footpath in the valley, always busy with runners and walkers. Today we are walking it clockwise. The well-maintained footpath skirts the water's edge and threads its way through the narrow belt of oak/beech woodland. It's overcast but pleasant enough to entice walkers with dogs, mums with push chairs and runners in hi vis Lycra. The recent spell of hot weather has reduced the water level so that there is a brown stony shelf around the shoreline where one or two lone fishermen stand, their rods extending hopefully into the water. A flock of some forty greylag geese graze and preen on a flat grassy shelf beside the overflow channel. The narrow belt of woodland along the shore is full of summer birdsong but the unmistakably striking and confident song of a thrush from a nearby branch breaks through all the others. It's quite a while since I've heard this instantly recognisable songster as song thrushes are nowhere near as numerous as they were and it reminds me of Browning's words:

> That's the wise thrush.
> He sings each song twice over
> Lest you should think he never could recover
> That first, fine, careless rapture

– although Gerard Manley Hopkins captures better the slightly piercing, rough edge of the song:

> The thrush, through the echoing timber
> Does so rinse and wring the ear,
> It strikes like lightening to hear him sing.

The wet winter, warm spring and recent rain have spurred the plants into such lush growth as I can ever remember. Each side of the path is lined with jungle-like growth of plants and flowers tumbling over and amongst one another in self-sewn herbaceous borders. Towards the back tall foxgloves, hogweed, ox-eye daisies and cow parsley provide an animal-themed backdrop, brambles and wild raspberries promise a rich harvest to come and sweet honeysuckle climbs over everything. Blue and yellow vetches sprawl along the footpath edge, with wood sage and that evil smelling dead nettle known as 'Stinking Roger'. It's all a complete delight though I'm sure that the 'keep fitters' pounding along the trail plugged into their devices don't even notice.

On the first Sunday in December the roads around Damflask are closed for the annual 'Percy Pud 10k' race, an event which has been run since 1993 following a proposal by Sheffield's Lord Mayor that clubs should put on special events during the year to celebrate the centenary of Sheffield becoming a city in 1893. Such is its popularity that entries have had to be limited to three thousand and huge sums are raised every year for charity. In this curious Christmas themed race all finishers receive a Christmas pudding instead of the usual medal!

How many times a day do we go through this routine, 'Let's have a cup of tea'? Turn on the tap and fill the kettle, easy as that, with never a thought of where the water actually comes from and how it reaches us so conveniently. We should, however, thank Victorian engineers every time we turn on the tap. The reservoirs and their works that changed the landscape of these valleys for ever, are an engineering marvel that we very rarely, if ever, consider. The most prominent are the huge embankments that hold back millions of gallons of water but beneath the hills are a complicated interconnected pattern of water mains and tunnels. These works have transformed the lives of people during the last two centuries.

By the mid-nineteenth century the need for a sustainable supply of clean water to the burgeoning population of Sheffield had reached the critical stage. The old dams on Crookes Moor, where the University now stands, could no longer cope with demand. The insanitary state of the town was appalling. Open drains and rivers polluted with sewerage, where the cholera bacillus found a ready breeding ground, contributed to shocking health statistics, especially amongst those living in the squalid back-to-back cottages in the poorer areas of the town. The 1832 cholera outbreak killed over 400 who lived in these areas. When the authorities turned their attention to supplying a clean water supply Sheffield, unlike cities such as Manchester and Birmingham, that had to look to the Lake District or Wales for their water supply, had an advantage in that its tributary valleys provided ideal conditions for water gathering and storage. By the 1840s the Redmires dams on the upper Wyming Brook and then the two Rivelin dams had been constructed, providing a supply of water to the town, although only reliably three times a week. Between these times household water then had to be stored in tanks or cisterns. It was not until the Loxley's reservoirs were functional in the 1870s that the supply became constant.

By the sound of it the name 'Damflask' would appear to be a very appropriate one for a reservoir but in fact it is simply the name of the small village that stood on this spot before the dam wall was built and before the valley was flooded between here and Bradfield. The hamlet consisted of two mills, Damflask Corn Mill and Damflask Paper Mill, a pub called The Barrel and a couple of farmsteads, clustered below the bridge that connected the two sides of the valley. Where the village stood now lies deep beneath the water about a hundred yards from the embankment, opposite the sailing club. Unlike other more recent drowned villages like Ashopton and Derwent over the hill there was no need to demolish the village as the buildings had fallen prey to the pounding force of the flood a couple of years previous to the construction.

On the night of the flood in March 1864 most of the villagers had a near miraculous escape. They were the only people lucky enough to have received any warning of impending doom when, earlier on that evening, a lad called Stevenson Fountain, whilst galloping down the valley to fetch the chief engineer to examine the ominous crack in the embankment of the Dale Dyke dam, stopped at The Barrel to repair his horse's bridle and mentioned the reason for his urgent late evening errand. Most villagers heeded the warning that passed from one to another and were able to move with their animals to higher ground. But not all. John King, Charles Platts, William Longden and a boy called John Ibbotson were working all night at the Shaw's Wire Mill, drawing out the thin wire that would be used to make fashionable crinoline dresses, and were carried away having not heard the warning, and 'Sheffield Harry' a navvy on the construction of Agden reservoir, drowned not having believed it could be true.

There was a narrow escape for Mrs Kirk with whom 'Sheffield Harry' lodged, for when she heard the alarm and rushed out of her house and across the bridge in her nightdress she suddenly remembered her cat and dog and turned back for them. With the cat under one arm and the dog under the other she just made it back across the bridge in time to see her house and the bridge itself torn down. In the days to come flood visitors to the site would be offered an unlikely photograph purporting to be of the lady and her pets as a memento of their ghoulish visit. As we stand here beside the road that crosses the top of the embankment, admiring the vista across the water and beyond to the surrounding green hills, it's difficult to imagine the horror of the events that overtook the little settlement that stood a few yards in front of us on that night, a hundred and fifty years ago, as the villagers watched their cottages, farms and mills being swept away in the torrent.

Monster Pike

I can't verify this, it but they say that if you go to Damflask reservoir on a hot summer's day and look over the wall here you will be able to see a lot of pike just under the surface. In October 2009 the *Yorkshire Post* published a report on *'the hunt for the 'real monsters of the deep.'* They were following up stories of a gigantic pike lurking in the 100ft deep reservoir that attacked a pet terrier that had gone in to cool down on a hot summer's day, and that had also tried to bite through the keep-nets of match fishermen and devour the thrashing contents. I wonder if the following posting on a fishing forum in 2006 might help explain the presence of such fish in Damflask?

> My hubby and I released a pike weighing 27.05 lbs into Damflask
> over 17 years ago, which he had caught while fishing Marshalls pond
> at Loxley. We had spent the day there and caught it just as it was
> going dusk. We took it up to Damflask wrapped up in the back of
> the van and spent about an hour reviving it before it swam off. God,
> it was scary for me with it thrashing about that night in the van. We
> took it up to Damflask because the owner at Marshalls pond didn't
> want it putting back in, as he was fed up of having to restock due
> to the pike eating his fish. We could have killed it, but thought we
> would give it a chance of life by moving it to other waters…

A fisherman's tale?

There have certainly been fisherman's reports of 40-odd-pound pike caught at Damflask then released straight back into the water and the very suggestion that the biggest pike in Britain could be lurking somewhere in this reservoir has attracted anglers from across Yorkshire and the Midlands to fish these waters. Record pike are not the only attraction either. Recent catches suggest that a record-smashing 10lb-plus chub could be caught here and there are known to be bream in the region of 20lb, which is the British record. Recent catches of 5lb-plus perch are edging close to making history. But it's the pike that make the adrenalin flow for many anglers. *"They are quite clever,"* says Mark Green, who runs the Selby branch of the Pike Anglers' Club, one of the dam-side anglers hoping to land a new British record pike. *"When you empty your net the pike are waiting to pounce like sharks."* Indeed, one pike had just guzzled a fish he was in the process of reeling in, *"I reeled in a roach one day and this pike came up and bit it straight off the line. There was this big swirl, and the pike was gone. It didn't half make me jump."* On the other side of Damflask, another pike fisherman has arrived. James Kitson has driven south from Wetherby to try his skill at catching 'The Big One'. *"The biggest I've caught so far is a 15-pounder but I love the thought that I could double that with my next cast. And the one after that, potentially, could hook the biggest pike in Britain and get me in the record books!"*

A Curious Barn

The footpath along the side of Damflask leads me to Low Bradfield, busy as usual with day trippers queueing at the ice cream van. An interpretation board in the car park on the other side of the cricket field marks the beginning of the walk round the next reservoir, Agden, which stands not on the Loxley but just to the north, filled by the water flowing down Agden and Emlyn Dykes. Leaving the village to follow the trail I notice for the first time the village name-stone that stands beside the road. It's a heavy chunk of local gritstone into which a charming depiction of a heavy horse with a plough has been carved in low relief, the features and lettering now picked out in emerald green moss. It's a delightful reminder of the local pride in the heritage of the community.

Ahead, after turning right up Windy Bank, there stands a huge abandoned stone barn a little way into the field on the left, derelict and overgrown with brambles and elder bushes. Set into the stonework of the barn wall is a very carefully engraved plaque which bears the words;

1826

Rebuilt at the Curates

sole cost.

Nemo soli sibi

Natus

Surely this must be the most obscure curiosity of the valley! It turns out that the same quotation, *Nemo soli sibi natus (Nobody is born for himself alone)*, was also placed over the church door in Ecclesfield in 1695. In Eastwood's *The History of the Parish of Ecclesfield: In the County of York* we read that:

> *Vicar Edward Mansel rebuilt the parsonage-house in 1695, over the door of which he placed this inscription, which, or a copy of it, is still just within the entrance of the present Vicarage:*

>
>
> *Edward Mansel. Vicar 1695.*
>
> *Nemo Soli Sibi Natus.*
>
> *Vivat Rex.*
>
> *Floreat Ecclesia.*
>
>

> *He also gave £50 towards building a parsonage at Bradfield.*

The words appear to have their origin in the fourteenth chapter of the book of Romans in the New Testament: *"For none of us liveth to himself, and no man dieth to himself,"* which in the Latin Bible appears as *"Nemo enim nostrum sibi vivit, et nemo sibi moritur."* Presumably the plaques in Ecclesfield and Bradfield are meant to remind us all that we should not keep our blessings to ourselves but share them with others for the benefit of the whole community.

This is all well and good and entirely appropriate for an inscription on a schoolroom or chapel, but on a barn? The secretary of the Bradfield Historical Society explains it in this way:

> It is my understanding that the inscription goes back to the time before there was a rector at Bradfield St. Nicholas and a curate would come either from Hathersage or Ecclesfield and was put up for the night or couple of days at Fair House Farm, since demolished, and in recompense for his keep at the farm gave money for the building of the barn at his own expense.

Quite some outlay for a few nights' lodgings I would have thought!

February 12th 2020, Agden

Agden reservoir is to my mind the most picturesque of the bodies of water in the valley. The path around the reservoir tracks through the oak and conifer woodland along the water's edge. Blue sky, the oaks, birches and hollies that line the far shore, backed by dark conifers, and the hills rising behind, are mirrored in the calm water, recalling birthday card watercolour scenes of the Lake District or Scotland.

As I follow the lakeside path there's a sudden raucous calling. The quiet is broken by a party of twenty greylag geese that have suddenly decided to descend from the field below the church, where they were quietly grazing, to tumble in a honking mass onto the lake. Wave after wave follows. 'Gaggle' strikes me as such an appropriate word to describe this raft of gregarious birds. Through the binoculars I spot an unexpected visitor to the lake. A cormorant, curiously out of place so far inland, stands on a mooring buoy in the centre drying his wings in the morning sun... and overhead a buzzard circles on outstretched wings, mewing to his mate.

The steep-sided side valleys that lead down from the moorland would originally have been naturally wooded, mostly a mixture of broad-leaved trees such as oak, birch and holly but also some yew. The deep clough of Agden Dyke still holds a remnant of this ancient woodland; the name Agden, originally 'Aykeden', meaning 'valley of the oak trees' is Old English or Anglo-Saxon, pointing to this long-standing woodland heritage. The footpath follows the steepening valley of the Agden Dike through the oak and rowan woodland as the reservoir narrows. A signboard tells us that the sloping field to the right of the path is Agden Bog, maintained by the Sheffield Wildlife Trust. It seems to be an important site for plants and insects but at this time of the year it has little of interest. I'll come back in the summer.

The narrow belt of Scots pines planted around the edge of Agden create an attractive backdrop to the water, as well as shady picnic spots, but the thick, dark coniferous plantations that were planted during the interwar years to provide future timber, in particular pit props, in uniform blocks that run up the hillsides, are less attractive. Having had little maintenance and being too close together the trees are weak and spindly and of little economic or environmental value. Now, as part of the Heritage Funded 'Sheffield Lakeland Partnership', Sheffield Council, working with Yorkshire Water and Sheffield and Rotherham Wildlife Trust, is coordinating a four-year programme of forestry work to thin or remove the conifer plantations around both Agden and Dale Dyke, and replant them with a range of broadleaf tree species that will benefit wildlife. The unmistakable raucous buzz of chainsaws within the Rocher End plantation on the eastern hillside above Agden, jars the peace and quiet. Much of the hillside has already been clear-felled to produce a mixed habitat of conifers, native broadleaves and cleared areas to support wildlife and birds such as willow tit, fly catcher, nightjar and goshawks but until the woodland regenerates it is a scene of devastation.

At this time of the year the ancient oak woodland further up the clough is awakening from the winter. Oaks and hollies, birches and rowan of all ages, shapes and sizes emerge from a sea of rusty coloured bracken fronds on the hillside though, in the steep, damp, sunless ravines of the Emlyn and Agden Dykes, the ferns are green and fresh. Strong sunlight slants through the trees and I spot the first peacock butterfly of the year, drowsy from winter sleep. Beside the path, overgrown and green with lichen, stand a pair of worn stone gateposts leading to nowhere. An elderly couple are sitting on a bench beside the path. They say that they drive up the valley every week to replenish the seed in the dozen or so bird feeders hanging from the low branches of a nearby oak. We sit and watch quietly whilst a colourful stream of tits, finches and nuthatches, as well as the inevitable marauding party of grey squirrels, tuck into the welcome winter feast. Suddenly a tiny bank vole darts out of a hole in a tumbledown stone wall, grabs a seed and vanishes again.

A few yards further along a low wall around a clear, flat area like a platform gives a further clue to former occupation. Here stood Agden House. A huge yew tree and a small ruinous stone building stand testimony to its former presence but the site is rapidly being engulfed by overgrown rhododendrons. It's difficult to reconcile the delightful nineteenth-century Agden House in the 1911 photograph, that stood here in the middle of the wood until the 1970s, quaint with its carefully clipped shrubs and tended gardens, with the scene today. It was formerly a hunting lodge and had been sold by the Duke of Norfolk to a Major Wilson from Riseholme in Lincolnshire at auction in 1885. The estate included 323 acres of grouse moor, woods, a rabbit warren, arable and pasture land, a quarry, trout streams and the fishing rights to Agden reservoir, as well as the house and gardens with their private carriageway. It was occupied throughout most of the nineteenth century by the Bramall family, Nicodemus, whose grave we have seen in Bradfield churchyard.

The house and surrounding land was sold by the major in 1945 to Sheffield Corporation Water Works and was divided into two cottages and rented to two families, one being Uttley and the other Hall. They continued to live there until it was decided to demolish it. Agden House was one of the many farms and lodges of the upper valley that fell victim to the policy of the water company of buying up properties that skirted the reservoirs and demolishing them in order to prevent pollution to the water supply. Nearby Frost House was pulled down in the 1950s, Rocher Head Farm was demolished in the early 1960s, and Agden House in 1972. At the time of the proposed demolitions a number of local people barricaded themselves into these properties as a protest but to no avail and the demolition took place rapidly to prevent further incident.

Air-Raid Precautions

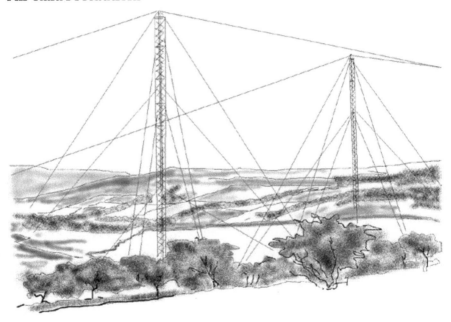

Prior to the growth of so many trees, Agden House had a clear view down the valley and over the reservoir. Standing where I'm standing now, the residents during the last war, the Buckley family, disturbed by the noise of aeroplane engines, stood in front of the house, watching as wave after wave of enemy bombers rained death and destruction on Sheffield in the distance and saw the sky alight with its burning. Mary Buckley, later Nun, in an interview for a BBC Radio programme, recalled this event of December 12th 1940 and went on to relate her memories of measures that were taken to protect the reservoirs from enemy action during the Second World War. *"As most people know, when Britain decided that the way to incapacitate the German production line was to breach their reservoirs using the so-called 'bouncing bombs', the Langsett, Ewden, Bradfield and Derwent Reservoirs were used for practice runs."* It turns out that Guy Gibson, the famous pilot who led the 'Dam Busters' command stayed at nearby Broomhead Hall to oversee the practices. Following the successful bombing raids on the German Reservoirs, however, it was feared that reprisals would take place, and Bradfield's four reservoirs were considered vulnerable. It was said, probably with some exaggeration, that if the reservoirs were breached Sheffield's armament-producing capacity along the lower Don Valley would be wiped out within fifteen minutes.

So a defence strategy was put into action to protect the dams. The first step was to erect huge masts about 100 feet high on either side of each reservoir, connected across the water by strong wires from which weighted wires were hung. These would prevent German bombers from flying low enough to bomb the reservoir embankments. This was a considerable enterprise considering that over twenty pylons were built altogether and each weighed twenty-five tons with the wire ropes adding another five tons. Secondly smoke generators were positioned around the sides of reservoirs, so that, in the event of an alarm being sounded, 30,000 smoke generators would pump a smokescreen across the water to hide them from above. It was said to be so effective that within five minutes the whole valley could be shrouded in impenetrable smoke! A contingent of 5000 troops, bivouacked beside the reservoirs, was responsible for maintaining the smoke installation and manning a battery of anti-aircraft guns. It is said that in case all this failed and the dams were breached dozens of boats had been strategically positioned down the Loxley Valley to rescue people from flooded homes. As far as I'm aware these elaborate precautions were never tested. It took the full year of 1954–55 for the towers to be dismantled and used as scrap iron at Samuel Fox's Stocksbridge steelworks.

Mary went on to recount her recollections of the so-called Strines Decoy, an area of some ten acres of ditches across the moorland filled with tinfoil and oil:

Following the air raids on Sheffield, the authorities decided to make a 'mock village' on Emlin Moors, about a mile beyond our farm. The purpose of this was that when enemy aircraft were expected a unit from the Defence Regiment would go onto the moors and light powder charges and make the enemy think that they were bombing a large area. This proved to be unsuccessful on two counts, one being that the Germans had far better surveillance and navigation aids than the British thought, and secondly the Defence Regiment could not find their way up onto the moor in the dark.

July 11th, 2020, Agden Bog Nature Reserve

I promised myself that I'd come back in the summer to see if I can spot some of the special plants that are supposed to flower here. It's a rare example of what is classed as a 'lowland raised bog', the vast majority of which have been drained and their unique ecology destroyed in recent years. The Wildlife Trust manage this reserve by grazing cattle on it during the winter to control the growth of invasive grasses and I must say that the regime certainly seems to be working; the whole field is studded with the spikes of orchids in every shade from pink to purple. From the adjoining footpath it doesn't look much, just a sloping field, backed by birch trees, but as I begin to cross it it's clear that it's like a sponge, with mossy tussocks of feathery grass and heather emerging from shallow pools and flowing water. In the wettest area, at the top of the field, I'm thrilled to discover two plants that I've never seen before, two of the most iconic plants of habitats like these, sundews, growing on a cushion of sphagnum moss, and bog asphodels, their starry yellow spikes shooting amongst tall reeds. I'm surprised, having only ever seen them in pictures, by how tiny the sundews are, no more than a couple of centimetres across. Their stems and fleshy 'fingers' around each leaf are bright pink. As the sun comes out every sticky droplet on the ends of each tentacle becomes a shining dewdrop, and I now realise why they are called sundews. Then I notice a patch of something completely unexpected, a very low growing plant with round green leaves no bigger than a sixpence and pink bell-like flowers that point upwards like goblets. I've never seen it before, and I can't relate it to any plant that I know. When I look it up later I discover that it's called bog pimpernel. It's been a magical morning.

October 25th 2020, Agden

It's precisely one full year since I began recording walks for this book; one long lockdown year during which it's kept me going when holidays have been cancelled. Today the bright autumn Sunday sunshine following grey weeks has brought out the crowds to Bradfield as I've never seen before. Last week's gusty northerly winds have already stripped the ashes but the rusting beeches around Agden Reservoir have come into their own. The sun slants through their grey trunks lining the water works driveway, casting dark shadows across the fallen leaves on the fern-lined path. As it strikes the orange and russet leaves remaining on the trees they glow with an almost translucent luminescence. I can't imagine anything that could brighten the mood and lift the soul like this glad sight and a sudden gust releases a flurry of multicoloured confetti in a tickertape welcome.

Amongst the leaf litter on the woodland floor one or two strangely coloured shapes have emerged like other-worldly organisms; toadstools of various kinds. Towards the water's edge there's one that's immediately recognisable, a bright scarlet cap with a white stalk, the classic fairy-tale fungus, well known for its poisonous properties – Amanita muscaria, one of the very few of the thousands of species of fungus with a common name, the fly agaric. Nearby, beneath a huge horse chestnut tree, I discover a quite different and even more unusually colourful fungus. At first glance I mistake it for a Cadbury's wrapper and it's not surprising as it's unusual to come across a bright purple living organism. Every part of the fungus, the stalk and the top, which resembles an upside-down frilly skirt, are bright violet colour. Later, on looking it up in my *Oxford Book of Flowerless Plants*, I discover that it's Laccaria amethystea, the amethyst deceiver, though I can't imagine how it got the name. Dead and dying branches of birch trees throughout the wood are host to bracket fungus of various kinds, some with wavy edges and others like woody plates and a ginger coloured jelly-like mass like wrinkled ears sits on a nearby branch. It's a shame that more varieties of fungus don't have common names because then we could get to know them better and begin to recognise their value and importance in their ecosystem.

I'm stopped short by a short, sharp 'kek' cry across the water. It's higher in pitch than a moorhen and I don't recognise it. I scan the dark water through the binoculars, and I'm delighted to spot a flotilla of over twenty brightly coloured mandarin ducks beneath the branches of a beech tree overhanging the other side of the lake. Both the sexes are very attractive birds but the males, with their unlikely tufts and sails of blues, reds and oranges are strikingly showy. Their colours match perfectly the oranges and russets of the beech leaves. Mandarins do not usually congregate in large flocks and a collection as large as this is most unusual. They cruise backwards and forwards, ducking and splashing, clearly attentive to the fewer female ducks. Most of mandarins' breeding activities take place at this time of the year, as soon as males emerge from their eclipse plumage in late September or early October, so it's clear why this raft of birds has congregated. Their calls and the sounds that they are making are even more curious than their plumage. Across the water comes a constant chatter, whistling, yelping, short high-pitched barks and a remarkable deep-pitched, throaty grunting sound that I can only compare with the boom of a bittern in being weirdly directionless. I can't spot which birds are making it as they seem to do it with closed beaks. Maybe it's part of the courtship display. Sights like this are relatively recent. Mandarins, as their name suggests, are native to the Far East but were introduced into parks and wildlife collections in this country from which they have escaped and became established in the wild. Unlike our native ducks, mandarins roost in trees, feeding on nuts, particularly acorns, chestnuts and beech mast, and they nest in holes in tree trunks, so Agden, with its fringing oaks, beech and alders is an ideal habitat. Here's an alien, introduced species that we can welcome and enjoy.

March 2nd 2020, Dale Dyke

There is no footpath along the Loxley from Low Bradfield to the third reservoir, Dale Dyke. The narrow Dale Road winds along the wooded riverside, passing Haychatters Farm, which I remember as 'The Haychatters', a remarkably remote little pub that began life as 'The Reservoir' serving the Victorian navvy dam builders. Just above Walker House Farm, with its three-bay cruck barn against the road, an interpretation board stands at the start of the footpath that leads around Dale Dyke reservoir. It recounts the story of the tragic event that occurred on this spot 156 years ago. Much of the thick coniferous plantation that was planted on the site of the stricken embankment here has already been felled and it's now possible to pick out a line of small white concrete marker stones, each bearing the letters C.L.O.B. Who would have guessed that these enigmatic memorials mark the site of the greatest dam burst disaster in English history? The letters stand for 'Centre Line of Bank', marking the original position of the first Dale Dyke embankment that failed so dramatically in 1864.

A couple of hundred yards further on I reach the top of the present Dale Dyke embankment and look over the expanse of dark, choppy water that stretches away up the valley. Until you stand here on a grey, cold March day like this, you can have no real appreciation of the enormity of what happened back then. What strikes me is the sheer bravado of those Victorian engineers and navvies who dared to construct such a colossal earthwork, rising a hundred feet above the valley floor, between these remote hillsides, in the misplaced certainty that it would hold back 700,000,000 gallons of water. Beside me, at the end of the embankment, stands some sort of monument, curved stone that looks like horns, and a stone plaque, inscribed to the memory of those who drowned when the original construction collapsed in 1864, held between them. It's only later that I discover that this was created by Andrew Vickers from 'Stoneface' and is supposed to represent the hollow in the dam wall that failed.

This February has been the wettest on record and today there is a loud roar as water thunders down the overflow weir at the far end of the dam wall. A party of plovers on rapid wingbeats heads arrow-straight over the reservoir up the valley towards the moorlands. From the moor above comes the unmistakable burbling call of a curlew, recently arrived back on the moor, heralding hope that spring is to come. I cross the quarter of a mile along the top of the embankment, intending to walk clockwise around the reservoir, but find that the gate to the bridge at the far end across the overflow is locked. I retrace my steps and follow the right-hand bank that winds its way about a mile or so along the tree-lined waters' edge. Across the water the left bank and the moorland above present a uniform dark, sombre slab of conifers whilst the waterside walk on this sunny side weaves its way through alders, oak and birch trees that provide shelter from the cold wind. The reservoir is so full that the water, that in the welcome sunshine reflects a rich deep blue, laps around their roots and branches.

The Collapse of the Embankment, March 11th 1864

We're becoming all too familiar these days with the misery caused by flooding. A year ago the Don overspilled its banks downriver, devastating the lives of hundreds of residents from Rotherham to Fishlake, some of whom are still not back in their homes. But to hear of a flood in which 250 people drowned and 4357 houses were flooded within the course of a single night is surely unimaginable. Yet a scenario that could easily have resulted in such a disaster was played out on out television screens in August 2019 and disaster was only averted by the last-minute intervention of hundreds of engineers and troops to shore up the stricken dam wall of the Toddbrook reservoir, above the town of Whaley Bridge, a few short miles west of the Loxley Valley. As it was built to virtually the same design as the Dale Dyke embankment, the parallels are striking. The alarm was raised by the manager of the local bowling club, who has a direct view of the dam from his home, and police officers and firefighters raced to the reservoir. As it quickly became apparent that 1.2 million tonnes of water could engulf schools, homes and businesses in the towns of Whaley Bridge and New Mills, thousands of residents were evacuated from their homes. Five times more water was going in than could be pumped out. It could have failed at any moment and the town of Whaley Bridge wiped out within hours. The disaster was only averted when an RAF Chinook helicopter was drafted in to drop hundreds of bags of sand and aggregate to shore up the collapsing embankment whilst massive pumps gradually drained the water behind it to a safe level.

Rewind over 160 years to 1853 when the Act of Parliament giving permission for the Sheffield Waterworks Company to proceed with 'The Bradfield Scheme' of three new reservoirs to be constructed in the upper Loxley Valley was passed, heralding the complete transformation of the landscape. It was not until 1859 that work began on the site of the embankment of the first, the Dale Dyke reservoir. Hundreds of 'navvies', many of whom had previously worked on the Woodhead rail tunnel to the north, tramped to the construction site with their tools, spades, pickaxes, barrows and the like, and set about digging a huge trench across the valley to form the foundation for the puddled clay wall on which the integrity of the colossal wall depended. This was an earth dam, built up layer by layer over the next four years to support the clay core, until it spanned the quarter mile width of the valley and stood 100 feet above the floor.

Quite probably detailed geological reports today would have indicated that this was exactly the place not to build such a colossal structure. Samuel Hammerton, the farmer at Walker House Farm which stood directly in line with the northern end of the embankment, knew the ground well. Just below the farm there was abundant evidence that the ground was not solid enough to support such an enterprise for, running diagonally across the road and down to the bed of the river, the line of an old land slip was marked by rough, disturbed ground. Initially the engineers proposed to build the embankment on this very spot but a test shaft revealed that the ground was broken up *'like a mass of shifting quicksand'*, it was said, and consequently the puddle trench was dug a little way further up. The locals were never entirely convinced of its safety and had the impression that the engineers were aware of the problem but were resolved to go ahead in spite of the risk as so much money had already been expended. Joseph Ibbotson, a neighbour from Bradfield, was later to report to the inquest at the end of March his observations subsequent to the disaster that seemed to suggest that their initial apprehensions had been justified. Large fissures had opened up adjoining the road and at Walker House Farm *"The flags on the floor are sinking in one part perpendicularly, as if one part of the building was standing on the solid and the other on sinking ground, the walls are cracked and the stone above the door head is broken,"* he reported.

The digging of the puddle trench, which would be later filled with impervious clay, was by no means straightforward. Springs of water constantly issuing from the exposed rocks necessitated the trench to be dug to sixty feet in places rather than the planned forty feet deep and two steam engines and three pumps worked day and night to stop it flooding. Even so, it was decided to commence filling it with puddled clay and gradually build up the clay wall, supported by earth and rubble on either side, until the whole embankment reached a hundred feet high and stretched a quarter of a mile across the valley.

By the end of 1863 the work was virtually complete and the reservoir had been filling. The weather during the winter of 1863–64, however, had been almost exactly the same as this last winter of 2019–20, continuously wet and stormy, and the reservoir had filled more quickly than anticipated. This had not particularly concerned the engineers who had every confidence in the structure, having built eight similar dams. They should have been concerned. Only twelve years previously the Bilberry reservoir at Holmfirth, only ten miles to the north, had failed in similar circumstances, resulting in the death of ninety-five people and causing appalling devastation. The engineer, George Leather, who happened to be the uncle of John Towlerton Leather, the chief engineer on the Dale Dyke project, was accused of 'culpable neglect and mismanagement'.

It was the farmer, Samuel Hammerton of nearby Walker House Farm, later to be killed in a railway accident, who was the first to spot the danger signs early on the fateful evening of Friday, March 11th, when he noticed a fifty-yard-long crack that ran along the outside of the completed embankment, some twelve feet from the top. The contractors were alerted and at first tried to reassure concerned neighbours that it represented no threat, although measures to relieve the pressure of water on the wall were enacted. The crack, however, was observed to be extending and widening. Late into the evening the chief engineer, John Gunsen, arrived on the scene and immediately appreciated the danger. Further emergency measures were hastily tried, including an attempt to blow up the waste weir with gunpowder, but to no avail. The ominous crack continued to grow until, a little before midnight, the huge earthwork suddenly collapsed releasing seven hundred million gallons of water, a hydraulic avalanche that tore down the valley with a noise like thunder. The force was unstoppable and anything that stood in the path of the deluge, mills, cottages, trees and bridges were smashed and swept clean away. No warning had been given and no danger apprehended by the sleeping people below.

The villagers at Low Bradfield were the first to experience the violent impact. Joseph Dyson's baby, only born the day before, was the first to die, washed out of his mother's arms in their cottage. The miller, Joseph Ibbotson, could only watch from his house a little higher across the valley as the ancient Bradfield corn mill exploded under the battering ram force and was carried away. *"This must be a wild dream, it cannot be reality,"* was his immediate impression.

The reporter Samuel Harrison resorted to wildly colourful imagery in his attempt to convey the enormity of the calamity:

> It seemed as if the bowels of the earth were being torn up, or as if some unheard-of monster were rushing down the valley, lashing the hillsides with its scaly folds, crunching up buildings between his jaws, and filling all the air with his wrathful hiss. Trees snapped like pistols, mills and houses stood and staggered for a moment and then disappeared in the boiling torrent. Not a trace of the well-built bridge remains, and of the large millstones and massive ashlar pillars of the three-storey mill nothing has been found.

On it swept, spending none of its energy but gaining power as the waters were funnelled down the narrow valley, gouging great holes in the banks as boulders were swirled round like ten-ton marbles. At Roebuck House William and Selina Marsden were woken by the noise and found the stinking brown water rising up the stairs. William quickly tore a leg from the dressing table and hacked a hole in the ceiling through which they both hoisted themselves and the baby onto the roof, from which freezing vantage point they saw that other neighbours had escaped in the same manner. At the hamlet of Damflask the bridge, the corn mill and the The Barrel disappeared. At Loxley Old Wheel fourteen-year-old Joseph Denton was carried to his death and the fate of William Bradbury the knife grinder at Rowel Bridge Wheel, has already been told. The village of Malin Bridge came in for a terrible battering. The farmhouse and outbuildings of the Trickett family were lifted up, demolished and rolled over, leaving only one portion of the stable wall standing amongst the ruin. Ten occupants of the house were lost, together with 102 of their neighbours.

On swept the flood water down the Loxley and Don towards Sheffield, smashing every bridge and destroying every mill in its path, flooding the courts and cottages of the poorest area of the Don Valley and drowning many in their beds. Hundreds of families were left destitute. Two hundred and forty victims are listed by Samuel Harrison, although this is almost certainly an underestimate. Their bodies were recovered from as far downsteam as Kilnhurst and Doncaster, 27 miles from the source of the flood.

And, standing as an eternal memorial to the event far more poignant than any piece of sculpture, we have a remarkably full photographic record of the scenes of the aftermath. Photographers were amongst the estimated fifteen thousand sightseers who flocked to the devastated Loxley valley in the following weeks, and those who came on the specially chartered trains to gawp could have their images recorded for posterity as they posed beside the 'picturesque' ruins of one or other of the shattered mills. Photography was still in its early days and it may well be that this is the first disaster ever to be recorded in this way.

Needless to say, the dam wall on which I'm standing today at Dale Dyke is not the same one that collapsed a quarter of a mile or so lower down. The building of the valley's four reservoirs proceeded with the completion of Damflask in 1867, Agden and Strines in 1869 and finally, despite the appalling tragedy that had occurred, Dale Dyke was rebuilt in 1875, an almost incredible achievement of only a little over ten years.

Carrying on my walk along the water's edge of Dale Dyke, in about a mile the reservoir narrows and I cross a bridge over the infant Loxley and climb the embankment to the top and look over the highest body of water in the valley, the Strines Reservoir. It's bleak up here. Right at the end of the embankment stands the only habitation visible, Broggin House, a grade 2 listed building set amongst the dark conifers with the date 1718 inscribed in the lintel. The name 'Strines', meaning a meeting of a stream or rivulet, dates from as early as the thirteenth century, when it was mentioned in the Sheffield Court records as the 'Water of the Strynd', referring to the stream that rose on the moors at the top end of Bradfield Dale and flowed down the valley to join the Loxley. The wide moorland bowl feeding the river's headwaters, with Strines Reservoir in the centre, in medieval times comprised Hawksworth Frith, the hunting demesne of the lords of Hallamshire. Apart from the present absence of trees it can't have looked much different all those years ago for the farm buildings that occupied these moorland intakes during the seventeenth and eighteenth centuries have been demolished in the interest of preventing contamination of the water supply to the reservoirs and their farmland has reverted to moorland. This open moorland stretches from the other side of the reservoir, and on the hillside, silhouetted against the sky, stands a sentinel; Sugworth Tower, better known as 'Boot's Folly'. From here its looks for all the world like one of the Stannington 60s tower blocks that stand guard at the opposite end of the valley.

August 29th 2020, Strines

Out of sight, tucked into a wooded dell just below the tower, stands the most imposing house in the upper valley, a great complex of eighteenth and nineteenth century gritstone buildings called Sugworth Hall. A house that stood here was first mentioned in the will of Robert Hawksworth in the 1560s and the Hawksworths were still at Sugworth until the early part of the eighteenth century. The deeds of the house suggest that amongst the well-known families of the upper dale there appears to have been an understandable pattern of intermarriage. In 1599 Grace Hawksworth of Thornseat Farm was married to Henry Worrell, in 1627 another Henry Worrell married Ann Hawksworth and in 1687 Robert Worrall married Ellen Hawksworth. It was these two families that held sway for hundreds of years in these remote parts; records of Sheffield Manor Court show that various branches of the Hawksworths were at Walker house Farm as well as Sugworth at least from the 1560s to the early nineteenth century, and the Worralls at Strines and at Upper House Farm, Ughill, for a similar length of time during which the families intermarried at least three times!

The hall at Sugworth was remodelled and extended during the nineteenth century, and by the late nineteenth century it was in the possession of Charles Henry Firth, of Riverdale House at Ranmoor, one of the wealthy Sheffield industrialists to be attracted by the local sporting opportunities. He was a younger son of Thomas Firth, the steel manufacturer, whose company would eventually become Firth Brown. Although Charles was involved with the running of the company it was his brother, Mark Firth, who, it is said, was the 'ruling and master spirit' and who built up the firm and served as Mayor of Sheffield. Today he is well remembered for his gifts to the city of Firth Park and the Firth Hall at the University.

After Charles died in 1892, the house passed to his widow and was bought by Philip Henry Ashbury managing director of Philip Ashbury and Sons, the silversmiths and electroplaters, who used it as a summer residence until his death in 1909. His son, George W. Ashbury, was to make the headlines by accusing two of his servants of stealing beds, bedding and towels, and was promptly sued for libel, his accusations costing him £15 in damages. After this, early in the twentieth century, the house became the home of civil engineer Charles Boot, son of Henry Boot who founded the family construction company and built it from nothing. Charles took over from his father just before the First World War, made a fortune from military contracts during the war and then continued to grow his wealth through post-war construction, particularly housing in Britain and on the continent.

Boot changed and extended the hall by adding a tower and battlements designed by the architect E. Vincent Harris, who was working with Boot on the construction of Sheffield City Hall in the late 1920s. During this time at the hall Charles Boot also constructed the nearby Bents House using stone from the nearby disused Bents Farm, Pears House Farm and Nether Holes Farm, which had all been demolished. Charles' great love was films and the early film industry. He developed a passionate desire to establish a film studio that would rival those in Hollywood and make Britain a big film producer, so he went off to Hollywood on a fact-finding mission. He returned within months with plans, which were to cost more than £1 million, to establish studios on the estate of Heatherden Hall, a large Victorian country house near Slough in Berkshire, which Boot had purchased in 1934; this was the start of the famous Pinewood Studios. On 30 September 1936, the studio complex was officially opened. The first chairman of the company was the millionaire flour-miller and film entrepreneur Mr J. Arthur Rank.

In 1929 the Boot family moved to Thornbridge Hall at Great Longstone in Derbyshire, although Charles' son Henry Matthew Boot continued to live at Bents House until his death in 1974. In 1934 Charles Boot sold Sugworth Hall to Colonel William Tozer, of the Hallamshire Battalion of the York and Lancaster Regiment, the grandson of Edward Tozer, one of the founders of steel manufacturers Steel, Peech and Tozer. He became Master Cutler in 1936, and invited Anthony Eden, Secretary of State for Foreign Affairs, to stay at Sugworth Hall following the Master Cutler's Feast ceremony at the Cutlers Hall. Boot died in 1945 and has an elaborate grave in Bradfield churchyard.

It was Charles Boot who built the 45-foot-high Strines Tower or Sugworth Tower or Boot's Folly, in 1927. It stands on a prominent eminence directly east of the house, in a hollow, embowered by trees. The footpath I'm following leads right past the tower but I'm not prepared to investigate too closely as it's surrounded by a herd of assorted cows and several have taken up occupation inside. It's a wonderfully curious and mysterious structure and the appearance of a black and white cow emerging from the doorway only adds to its quirkiness. It is obvious from close up that it was built using masonry from earlier buildings, probably leftover stone from the building of neighbouring Bent's House. The entrance has a seventeenth-century date stone and the windows of the lower storeys contain old mullions obviously extracted from elsewhere. The upper windows are by contrast, relatively modern, with metal frames. Today the interior is bare but originally it had elaborate wood panelling and a furnished room at the top where friends and family could enjoy the splendid view down the valley. A wooden staircase wound round the interior walls to the top to emerge onto the roof, but this was removed some years ago after, it is said, a cow, more adventurous than usual, climbed the stairs and couldn't back down. It was with considerable difficulty that the animal was eventually rescued!

Different stories are told of the reason for the tower's construction. It may have been built simply to provide work for the construction company's workmen during the difficult period of the depression but some say that Boot had the tower built so that he could see High Bradfield churchyard where his wife, Bertha, who had died in 1926, aged 56, was buried. Considering that he was remarried only five months later, to Kate Hebb, at St Peter's Church in London, this seems unlikely and the truth may be rather less romantic, that it was built by Boot simply to entertain his friends!

Some Curious Stonework

I had heard that somewhere near the tower there lay a stack of very interesting-looking pieces of masonry, carved pieces of stonework, presumably from some demolished building or other. Having spent some time searching in a wide circle around the tower I came to the conclusion that it must have been removed and set off walking away, down the footpath leading to Dale Dyke. It was only then that I almost stumbled across the stack of classically-carved pieces that lay partly concealed in the long grass, heather and bracken;

four or five six-foot-long sections of fluted pillars, a couple of finely carved round pillar heads, lintels and squared bases and a few scrolled tops of Ionic columns. I'm immediately reminded of elaborately iced wedding cakes!

What are we to make of them? Obviously great expense and effort was employed to get these weighty pieces to this remote spot. It seems unlikely that they were brought simply to be left here. Could it be perhaps that Charles Boot had designs on constructing another folly? As we know, he was in the habit of cannibalising older buildings to retrieve materials. Even more intriguingly, where did they come from? A number of internet sources inform us that:

> The stones are believed to have come from Brunswick Chapel which was at the bottom of Sheffield Moor. The chapel was bombed during the Second World War and Mr Boot was charged with making the chapel safe so brought some of the masonry to his house on the moors.

So, that's that. Not quite. In fact, I think that this is one of those stories that gets told once and has been accepted and copied time after time without question. The Brunswick Wesleyan Chapel was indeed a huge edifice that was built in about 1850 on South Street, now The Moor, in the city centre. Like many nonconformist chapels it certainly had a strictly classical façade. However, many photographs survive of the building and they very clearly show the relatively plain stonework, none of which matches the elaborately carved pieces at Strines. More than this, it seems that the chapel was not destroyed in the war, only damaged and stood derelict until the mid-1950s. A series of photographs clearly dated August 1956, taken by C.H. Lea, show the demolition and piles of masonry, including fluted sections of pillars, quite unlike the designs of these at Strines, lying amongst the debris. Even had the pieces been part of the Brunswick Chapel Charles Boot could not have had anything to do with their transport here for, by this time, Boot had long since left Sugworth, and he had died in 1945. We do know, however, that Boot's company earned the contract to demolish the stately home of Clumber in Nottinghamshire after it was destroyed in a fire in 1938 and that Boot rescued a large number of statues, fountains, and building facades from Clumber and installed them at his house, Thornbridge Hall, near Great Longstone in Derbyshire, where they still grace the gardens. But clearly this was after his time at Sugworth. An even more intriguing possibility is that the Strines pieces are actually some of the bits and pieces which came his way while the company were working on a huge land reclamation scheme in Greece! They do look remarkably like pieces of the Parthenon that litter the site of the Acropolis in Athens.

Having failed to solve the mystery of the discarded stonework I head down the steep, muddy path towards Dale Dyke. The late summer moorland stretches beyond Strines reservoir. Some years the heather lives up to its reputation and the moors are lit up at this time of the year with a spectacular purple haze, but not quite this year, when the colour tone is rather more subdued to a bronzy hue. I slip and slither down the path that the cows have churned into a quagmire. In places the mud is a bright ochrous orange, betraying the presence of iron oxides in the layers of rock below. Lower down the path levels out and follows the 'Sheffield Country Walk' a challenging 85.9 km (53.4 mile) circular route that takes you right round the outskirts of the city. This section is well maintained, with new gates and even an occasional picnic table.

In the days and weeks following the disastrous flood of 1864 special artists and correspondents were dispatched to produce reports and sketches for publication in the *Illustrated London News*. They were written as though the reports were coming from some far-flung outpost of the Empire but the accompanying engravings present us with a unique record of the landscape at this precise moment. The view '*showing the broken dam*' is particularly interesting, depicting as it does the route of today's walk along the opposite side of the reservoir. At that time the hillsides that are now cloaked with conifers were evidently more intensively farmed than they are today with fields neatly divided by well-maintained boundaries. In the intervening years many of the farms were abandoned, bought and demolished by the water company, and the conifer plantation created.

Above the plantation the footpath leads through open meadows across which the stone walls have tumbled and the hedges have grown out, creating two of the most delightful features along this footpath; the majestic trees that once were planted as hedges; oaks, ashes and a massive sweet chestnut, which, with a girth of 5.5 metres is listed in the Woodland Trust's inventory of Nationally Important Ancient Trees, and some extraordinary gateposts. Having once held wooden gates these posts still stand even though the hedges and gates are gone and the stone walls are reduced to mere bumps across the fields. They have acquired a sculptural, almost monumental, quality. Chiselled from a very hard gritstone every one is a different shape and size and they show signs of having been reused many times, as different sized and shaped holes, small square ones in patterns, round ones or occasionally triangular ones made for different purposes, have been laboriously drilled through different faces. Some stand straight and tall, one is roughly shaped and slightly twisted and some are rounded on one side. Some stand in pairs beside a lost gateway and some stand alone, unrelated today to anything else. How old are they? Where were they quarried? Who made them? – enigmatic questions that we can only ponder as we leave them behind and the footpath enters the plantation and down an apparently endless sequence of steps towards the water's edge of Dale Dyke and leads round below the embankment. Having crossed the river I follow the path back along the opposite hillside passing Hallfield and Broggin once more.

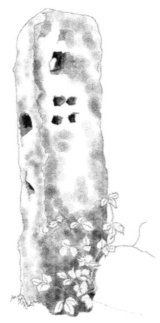

— 8 —

Across the Moorlands

The eye can never be weary of looking upon these lovely hills, for the daily rising and setting of the sun are pictures of ever recurring beauty. If the storms which sweep down the Dale are fierce and formidable they are also grand and majestic.

FROM A LIFE AT ONE LIVING (1884) BY REV ALFRED GATTY

July 26th 2020, Ughill Moor

The quickest way to access the head of the valley is not to follow the narrow, winding lanes along the Loxley but to take the A57 up the Rivelin Valley; the Manchester Road that leads over the Snake Pass. Towards the Derbyshire border the road passes Hollow Meadows, a strung-out, ragged group of houses and bungalows, and a more impressive stone building that was once Sheffield's school for delinquent and truant boys. Hollow Meadows, originally a sheep pasture of 347 acres, was 'Auley's Meadows' after the Hawley family, a name that has been altered over the centuries by a process of 'Chinese whispers'. A little further, just before the road dips down towards Derbyshire, is Moscar, a group of farms and a lone Methodist chapel, and here I turn right on Rod Side to follow Stake Hill Road, one of the old packhorse routes that cross the moors that was never upgraded and surfaced. I'd come up here to see if I could solve the mystery of something I'd heard about recently, a ruinous building on the top of the moor known locally as Ughill Castle, and I set out along the trackway as it curves away across the summit of Ughill Moor between gritstone walls. It's a timeless place, a wide sandy path that resounds to nothing more than the echoes of ghostly coach and horses until, that is, the peace and quiet is shattered by the roar of half a dozen orange Suzukis ridden by black leather-clad bikers!

Away to the left, at the highest point of the moor, I spot the ruin and head through the heather following a narrow sheep track towards it. Small orange butterflies, small heaths, lift from the tussocks and flutter skittishly in the stiff breeze before settling, immediately closing their wings. Wiry, black and white gritstone sheep stand and stare. The ruin stands on a shelf overlooking the upper valley. Dark conifer plantations reach up the opposite hillside above Strines Reservoir, and below stands Boot's Folly.

As I approach the so-called 'castle' it's clear that this building, whatever it was, had been built to last, with regular cut stone blocks, not like an old barn, and it's far too small to be the remains of a hunting lodge. The remains of the tumbled walls stand only to head height and fallen blocks lie piled around. Could this have been another of Charles Boot's building projects? It could be the base of another tower or even simply a picturesque ruin. Given what we know about Boot's interest in the film industry this seems possible. I'm satisfied that it was never a castle but I'm mystified that I can discover no records of it whatsoever.

Back on the old road the dry-stone walling along the left-hand side is well maintained whilst on the right only traces of it remain. The reason for this soon becomes apparent; the stone has been robbed to build a long line of well-built round grouse buts that stretch down this side of the moor, each numbered in white paint. In a couple of weeks' time this place, now deserted, will be alive with the shouts of beaters and the thwack of gunfire. But toffs in tweeds and gamekeepers are not the only people who can regularly be spotted up here in the middle of the moor. There is also an occasional enthusiast, scouring this moor above Ughill in the hope of discovering a few pieces of rusting metal. The little pieces of iron that occasionally turn up hidden amongst the heather are the only remains of an RAF aircraft, a Vickers Wellington T. Mk.10 MF627 of No. 6 Air Navigation School that unfortunately crashed here during the night of October 22nd 1952 whilst on a night navigation exercise from RAF Lichfield, Staffordshire. The plane was destroyed. Of the three who were on board that night the pilot, Sgt Reginald Keith, and one of the trainee navigators, Pilot Officer John Brian Sunley Thirkell, escaped with minor injuries but the other trainee, Pilot Officer David Edward Ward, was more seriously injured. All were incredibly lucky to survive at all. Over the years there have been many instances of aircraft coming to grief on the moorlands of the Dark Peak. It's partly to do with the general location. Even though there's more mountainous ground further north, here we're surrounded by heavily populated areas which during the Second World War and after were home to a number of airfields and there were regular flights across the Peak District, as well as plenty of aerial training like that undertaken in October 1952. Unfortunately inexperienced pilots, faulty equipment and bad weather took their toll.

Platts Farm and the Knights of St John

The moorland road down into the valley meets the lane that goes towards Ughill but before I reach the hamlet I turn to the right, following a lane that leads past Platts Farm. A little while ago Platts Farm came up for sale for £1,295,000. The estate agent's brochure contained the extraordinary claim that *"Platts Farm is believed to date back to 1347 when it was within the stewardship of the Knights Hospitallers of St. John of Jerusalem,"* which is such a very curious claim that I'm intrigued and can't resist investigating.

The stone-built farmhouse can be seen across the well laid out garden from the lane that passes buildings. It's very attractive and obviously recently tastefully renovated, but not particularly distinctive. But then I spot the carving of a diagonal cross on the underside of one of the stone kneelers on the edge of the stone-slabbed roof. There is evidence that this simple inscription may signify that the farm had a most curious medieval history. It appears that, prior to Henry VIII's dissolution of the monasteries, Platts Farm was held by the Manor of Waldershelf, a part of the great Chapelry of Bradfield, adjoining our valley to the north, and that, during the twelfth century, William de Lovetot, the Lord of the Manor of Hallamshire, granted Waldershelf Manor to the crusaders of the 'Knights Hospitallers of the Order of St John of Jerusalem'.

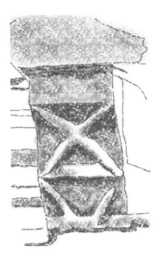

The Knights had established a brotherhood and hospital in Jerusalem for the care of sick and poor pilgrims in the eleventh century but, by the early twelfth century, they had been turned out of Jerusalem, the city having been retaken, and many had returned to Europe. The Order established a priory in England that received various endowments of land and, by the early fourteenth century, they owned over ninety manors throughout the country. There was a traditional belief, recorded by Joseph Hunter, that the knights held some twelve houses in our area, each displaying the cross on the principal building, like the one on Platts Farm, to indicate that it was exempt from tithes. We don't know how these properties came into the hands of the knights but by the time of Elizabeth I they had been taken by the crown and that, sometime between 1560 and 1590 the Manor of Waldershelf and the farmstead had been purchased by the Lord of the Manor, George Talbot, 6th Earl of Shrewsbury, to add to has (and his wife Bess of Hardwick's) extensive portfolio of lands and properties. The claim of the estate agents in their sales brochure that: *"The property has been home to historical figures including the Earl of Shrewsbury, Bess of Hardwick and the Duke of Norfolk,"* is, to say the least, most unlikely if not downright untrue, although it was owned by them.

The farm track continues between open hay fields for a mile or so before reaching the most remotely positioned farm in the valley, Crawshaw Farm, that sits at the focus of a wide moorland bowl at the head of Ughill Brook. The approach to the farm is heralded by the usual abandoned paraphernalia rusting away beside the lane, including a small, tracked, ancient rusty-red bulldozer embedded in the shooting grasses and weeds. The farm complex is huge, a number of colossal iron sheds stand opposite a modern house, built sometime in the 60s or 70s, incongruous in this setting, encircled by sheep-filled fields. The original farmhouse, a three-storey stone building with the house at one and the barn with arched threshing door openings at the other, only comes into sight as I begin to climb the moor above, where the hardy, dappled black and white moorland sheep pause to stare, and I pass over the ridge, where the footpath meets Rod Side.

A Macabre Mausoleum

A most curious house stands here, high on the ridge, overlooking the bleak moorlands at the head of the Rivelin valley. A rugged-looking, stone-built building, in the shape of a cross, with four gabled wings with windows on each protruding face. It's called Crawshaw Lodge which gives a clue to its origin as one of those fanciful Victorian buildings erected by wealthy Sheffield businessmen for their sporting pleasure, in this case by an industrialist named Horacio Bright. He came from a wealthy family of Jewish jewellers and became a prominent figure in the iron and steel industry. Bright's firm of Turton, Bright & Co made high quality steel dies for the Royal Mint. He had something of a reputation for pretentious eccentricity and would drive up to the lodge from his home in Sandygate, Sheffield, in a coach and four accompanied by liveried outriders. In 1891, Bright suffered a personal tragedy when both his wife and his only son, Sam, died within the space of five months.

This event resulted in the construction of the most macabre curiosity in the valley, an elaborate personal mausoleum which he had constructed in isolated splendour in the area of woodland adjacent to the lodge. Struck down with grief, he personally prepared the corpses of his loved ones for burial and furnished the interior of the square stone building luxuriously with paintings and fine furniture and had glass panels inserted into the lead coffins so that he could sit and gaze upon the faces of his loved ones. He had an organ installed in the building and rode out in his coach and four to spend evenings playing dirges to their remains, while his groom quietly got on with dusting the coffins. Two other buildings housed the remains of Horacio's parents and other family members. Four years later he was remarried to a young actress who bore him a son as a seventieth birthday present! In 1906, he too was buried in the mausoleum.

The ruinous remains of the building, cordoned off by iron railings, are hidden in a copse of trees, whose dark, intertwined branches give it an air of added mystery. In the 1980s vandals or thieves hoping to find buried treasure smashed through the steel doors. The furnishings were shattered and the coffins were smashed open. Strangely, it appears that the original coffins, with their glass windows, are now housed at Kelham Island Museum, less than a mile from where Bright's factory once stood, though I've never seen them on display.

In his book *Lest We Forget*, Douglas Lamb describes a visit he made to the Bright Mausoleum:

> The site is overgrown and derelict. There are two small buildings at
> the top of the hill, both of which are empty, together with a heap
> of rubble which may be the remains of a third building and five
> family gravestones set into the surface of a flat-topped, raised piece of
> ground amongst wind bent and stunted trees. Underfoot the ground
> is carpeted with weeds and lank grass. Even the iron gate, which
> is the only way in, is creaking with rust and disuse. It is altogether
> a desolate and God-forsaken place.

November 18th 2020, Mortimer Road

This morning I've driven past Moscar and the Derbyshire boundary sign on the Manchester road before turning right onto the minor road signposted 'Strines'. This road, that was originally another packhorse trail, snakes northwards, contouring across the heather moorland, to make its way towards Penistone and ultimately to Halifax, and for this reason it was originally known as 'Halifax Gate'. The road is narrow and winds its way around the head of the Loxley valley, diving steeply once or twice down wooded ravines and passing through acres of conifers. The views to the right down the valley, with the sun glinting on the waters of the Strines and Dale Dyke Reservoirs, are stunning.

This road became known as 'Mortimer Road', having been 'turnpiked' by an Act of Parliament that was enacted in 1771 at the expense of Hans Winthrop Mortimer, Lord of the Manor of nearby Bamford, who expected to reap large profits from the tolls that could be collected on the wagons carrying lead from the Peak District and woollen goods from the West Riding. Although there were other investors such as the Duke of Devonshire and Lord Melbourne, Mortimer bore the greatest financial risk, having raised £8,000 by mortgaging his Bamford estate. In the event the expected level of traffic did not materialise and the venture failed. Mortimer was bankrupted and died in poor circumstances in 1807. His legacy is this remarkable and delightful road. Since it's still as narrow as when it was a turnpike and doesn't link between any major towns it is generally quiet and used mainly by trippers.

Where the road crosses the ridgeline and descends to the Ewden valley to the north, stands a very distinctive milestone. This milestone, at the point where Mortimer Road meets the old Penistone Road, is dated 1740, so it was erected when the road was a packhorse route, before the construction of the turnpike road. It shows directions and distances to Penistone, five miles, Sheffield, nine miles, Hope, nine miles and Bradfield, two miles. If you were to drive to any of these destinations and record the mileage, you would discover that they are wrong by about 25%. In fact the distances on the milestone are in Yorkshire miles, the proverbial 'country mile', which measured ten furlongs, a customary measurement that was still being used in outlying areas like this long after the length of the mile had been set by statute in 1593 at only eight furlongs.

The Duke's Road

It's the quiet that strikes me as I get out of the car and lace my boots beside the milestone. I've left behind the background hum of the city, whose tall buildings distantly catch the slanting sun way below, and the only intrusion of noise is the occasional low-pitched drone of aircraft, their white trails converging on their long approach to Manchester Airport, way beyond the western horizon. Across the road a deep and wide ditch with a tall embankment to one side stretches across the watershed here between the Loxley and Ewden valleys. This mysterious and enigmatic feature is known as 'The Bar Dyke'. It was formerly considered to be an earthwork probably erected as a frontier defence either during the prehistoric or post-Roman periods, but David Hey considers that it actually marks the medieval boundary of Wigtwizzle Common that stretches over the valley to the north.

Setting off westwards I'm following the path known as 'The Duke's Road' across the open moorland. As I tramp along the steadily rising footpath the sun reflects tiny stars from the chips of quartz crystals that glint in the wet gritstone of the path and I can't resist picking up a few of the attractive quartz pebbles, most milky white, a few rose, others creamy, that have weathered out of the course rock, and I ponder on the millions and millions of years that they have taken to get here; eroded from quartz veins in some Scandinavian mountain 300 million years ago, tumbled and shaped by river and sea, before being dumped, buried and cemented into rock, to eventually surface again as they are released from their rocky bed by wind and water.

Standing proud of the heather on the moor are occasional rocks, rough, dark gritstone, wind-shaped and rounded. No tree up here, only undulating mounds of heather and bilberry. Looking back to the east four of the power stations on the Trent and Ouse, up to thirty miles away, are clearly visible, and in the binoculars, beyond these, stretch row after row of white turbines lined on each distant, hazy horizon away towards the Yorkshire Wolds. They say that the next highest spot to the east is the Russian Urals. I scan the furthest horizon for York Minster's towers but, as usual, it's not quite clear enough.

Around me calls of red grouse erupt suddenly. They resent my presence in their territory. A hidden bird is startled and explodes from the heather nearby with a sharp, repeated barking call, something between a cluck and a quack. There's a frantic flapping as it skims low over the moor before fanning its tail and wing tips to sail down further off, still clucking indignantly. Another stands alert on a rock. He's a handsome bird in finest winter plumage, not really red but a rich tawny brown with grey feathery legs, white eye makeup and a remarkable bright red fleshy crest above each eye. It's a flashy signal to any local females that he's an attractive mate. Fancy having sexy eyebrows! Across the moorland hillside rectangular and oval shapes appear to be cut into the heather, evidence of the way that the moorland has been managed to provide just the right habitat for the grouse to feed and breed. During the autumn months, even from areas quite close to Sheffield city centre, plumes of grey smoke billowing from the distant moors can be seen as areas of heather moorland are being burned in order to stimulate regeneration of the young shoots on which the young birds feed. I recall walking down towards Dungworth School one afternoon in late December to see our granddaughter perform in the annual nativity play. The sun was already low behind Derwent Edge at the head of the valley to the west. A huge plume of smoke, sickly grey tinged with the pink of the dying sun, arose from the moor and sank down into the valley. You could taste it.

In this annual maintenance regime lies the clue to why this wide track is called 'The Duke's Road'. The Duke in question is the Duke of Norfolk who, as Lord of the Manor of Hallamshire, was awarded some 5000 acres of moorland common at the head of the valley under the Ecclesfield Enclosure Act of 1811. Prior to this the moors were used as open grazing land and exploited for natural resources such as building stone, gannister, fire-clay and coal. This award, however, changed the access rights to the moors from common land used by local people to private hunting estates owned by the landed gentry. Hunting lodges were built and the moors were managed by gamekeepers and land agents specifically to suit the conditions for breeding grouse and other game. Heather was encouraged to grow and dominate the vegetation, managed by rotational burning, a process that has been carried out for over a hundred years and has had a major effect on the moor as we see it today.

It was early in the nineteenth century that the 'sport' of grouse shooting began to be carefully managed. In 1819 a Game Association was created with members paying an annual subscription of three guineas to shoot across the Duke's moors and a gamekeeper was appointed. The intensive management of the moorland was initiated for the benefit of grouse and public access to the grouse moors was increasingly restricted. An important change to the management of the moorlands under the 'Game Act' of 1831 meant that the right to kill game was available to anyone on the possession of a game certificate, enabling the landowner to rent out the shooting rights, and a new 'Bradfield Game Association' was created, with fifteen members paying £10 per annum and the treasurer given sole responsibility for the management of the shoot and the prosecution of poachers, without having to involve the police. It is said that some forty men were employed on the opening day of the season to protect the moor from illegal shooting.

Anyone who trespassed on the land in pursuit of game was now criminally liable. The penalties for night poaching were especially severe; on a first conviction imprisonment with hard labour for three months; on a second, imprisonment for six months, and for a third offence the offender was liable to imprisonment with hard labour. Amongst the artisans of Sheffield, however, were a number who appear to have regarded poaching as a worthwhile if hazardous sport. It was not unknown for encounters between the local owners of shooting rights and armed gangs of poachers to be violent and, occasionally, deadly. Thomas Heiffer in his little book of 1831, *Walks in the Neighbourhood of Sheffield* discovers this when he is caught out by a storm whilst walking up the valley from town and takes refuge in a hostelry somewhere around Bradfield. On becoming aware of three rather shifty looking characters he asks his companion;

> "Who are those three lads sitting together listening so eagerly to that tall fellow with long light gaiters, their white and black complexions have surely seldom been turned to the sun?"

> "You do not know the craftsmen of your own town?" replies his friend, "Observe their black aprons tinged with iron, tucked carefully under their vests. Tomorrow, long before it is light, those young gentlemen will make their first appearance on the moors. The oldest, you will observe, has the stock of a gun in his coat pocket and the younger is tightening the band by which he holds a young half bred dog."

As the grouse population increased the Association flourished. After the introduction of shooting buts in the 1860s heather burning was carried out far more systematically and the moors managed more intensively in order to provide enough birds for the increasing popularity of the sport, resulting in the moorland landscape we see today.

Although it provides an excellent habitat for the grouse, as well as moorland birds such as golden plover, curlews and wheatears, the practice of heather burning is now under scrutiny by environmentalists. They claim that it damages the unique fragile ecosystem of these upland bogs that rely on the mosses to act as sponges holding the rainfall and preventing potentially damaging run off. People have even pointed to it being a contributory factor in the disastrous flooding of the Don Valley in 2019. If this management regime were to be discontinued birch and conifers would regenerate and the ecosystem would be changed.

Amongst the grass tussocks beside the Duke's Road path, I spot some delicate white bones, clearly belonging to a bird. They have long since been picked clean and beside them lies the perfect skull of a curlew, that emblematic bird of the moorlands. The thin, curving beak is improbably long. It's a darker colour than the skull and tapers to a fine sensitive point. It will make a fine addition to my collection of bird's skulls. In the spring these waders will return to breed up here and the moors will resound again to their plaintive cries and piping whistles.

I had come up onto the moor in the hope of spotting another of its iconic birds, the short-eared owl, but the only raptors I spot today are a buzzard, lazily circling on outstretched wings, and a kestrel, the windhover, doing what it does best, keeping a steady station in the air whilst flickering wings and tail against the breeze, and I recite in my head Gerard Manley Hopkins' masterful evocation of the moment, "I caught this morning morning's minion, Kingdom of daylight's dauphin, Dapple-dawn-drawn Falcon, in his riding of the rolling level."

A little further on there's the remains of one of the moor's most celebrated creatures; a dead mountain hare; the 'snow hare'. The ears are considerably shorter than his lowland cousins' and, as it's November, his fur is just beginning to turn white from the belly and long legs, adaptations for survival in the harsh moorland winter. Except that, if it doesn't snow, this camouflage doesn't work and they are easily spotted scampering across the dark moorland vegetation. The local population of these beautiful animals is descended from releases in the northern Peak District made for sporting purposes in the 1870s and 80s and it's now the only population of mountain hares in Great Britain outside Scotland. Their numbers have been rising over the last thirty years or so and they have become a well-established feature of these moorlands, a familiar sight to hikers and walkers. It's not clear what killed this one.

After three miles of gradual ascent, I reach the flattened moorland summit. This is a different environment altogether, blanket bog. It's wet with standing pools everywhere and rivulets of brown peaty water crossing the path. There is no more heather, it's replaced by tussocks of course red grass and tall reeds shooting through emerald pillows of spongy moss. At this point I begin to understand why GHB Ward called this *"The loneliest, wildest walk in West Yorkshire."* Without the grey rectangular flagstones, carefully laid to extend the path across the boggy terrain by the Peak Park and Moors for the Future Partnership, I'd be in danger of sinking up to my knees at every step. Back in the 1920s Ward had to navigate the bleak featureless plateau without their benefit, and I'm sure that were he around today, being something of a purist, he wouldn't approve. The huge flat sandstone slabs that make up the path across the bog were originally engine blocks that supported the machinery in the cotton mills of Lancashire. Thousands of tons have been airlifted by helicopter to create miles of footpath across the moorland bogs like these that were threatened by erosion. They make a wonderfully easy surface to walk on as I approach my destination, the rocks of Back Tor on Derwent Edge.

Up here on Back Tor, at a little over 500 metres above sea level, the view over the Dark Peak moors and valleys opens. A toposcope or orientation table stands nearby to help identify distant landmarks. Immediately in front the land falls away, revealing the great Derwent Valley reservoirs of Howden, Derwent and Ladybower far below, and to the north paler and paler blue-grey moorland horizons stretch into the far distance of Bleaklow and beyond. Standing close to Back Tor is a prominent cairn of stones. It is known as 'Lost Lad.' The story that accounts for this curious name may or may not be legendary but there are entries in the burial register of Bradfield Church indicating that the eponymous 'Lost Lad' was far from the first to succumb to the harshness of the unpredictable weather that can all too suddenly overcome travellers in these uplands. A hand written note in the register for

August 25th, 1718, for example, records starkly, *"Memorandum-a coffin put in the earth with Bones of a Person found on the high moors, thought to be of Richard Steade."*

Lost Lad

The curious legend of 'Lost Lad' concerns a boy, Abraham Lowe, who ran a small farm with his widowed mother down in the village of Derwent, long before it was flooded by the waters of Ladybower in the 1940s. One winter when the village was cut off by heavy snowfalls and icy weather, Abraham's mother sent him off to locate the sheep and bring them back to the farm. With a cheerful wave, he set out up the hill towards Derwent Edge with his dog by his side. After the steep climb he left the valley and made his way to the snow-covered moorlands where he found some sheep and began to round them up. The weather however, was deteriorating. It began to snow and a thick mist came down. Before long, it was impossible to recognise any of the landmarks he knew so well. For hours he struggled through the ever-deepening snow and mist, but he was lost. The snowfall was now a blizzard, and Abraham crawled under a rock to shelter. Then he waited, hoping that the bitter weather would abate. But alas, it did not. He struggled to stay awake, but his eyelids kept shutting. Before he finally gave in to the exhaustion caused by the coldness he found a stone and scratched the words 'LOST LAD' on the rock. Then, frozen, weary and hungry, exposure to the elements claimed him and he fell asleep, never to wake again. It is said that, even after his death, his dog stayed with him until it too died.

Abraham's mother watched the high snow-covered hills from her farmhouse window, hoping to see her son descending but as night came on hope faded and the following morning she set out with her neighbours to search for the boy. They searched all day but they found no trace of him. Everywhere was pure white, the blizzard having wiped out any footprints. The search was resumed the next day, but in vain. Eventually the hope was abandoned and it was not until spring that another shepherd, spotting the words 'LOST LAD' scratched on the rock, found the remains of Abraham and his dog. He made a small pile of stones to mark the spot, and for over 100 years, every shepherd who passed added another stone. This grew into the huge cairn that can still be seen today near Back Tor. Another version of the story claims that the dog survived and stayed with the boy until his body was discovered and lived to be thirty-one years old! And that's not the end of the story, for, from time to time, people have reported seeing the ghosts of the lost lad and his sheepdog wandering in the winter snow.

July 7th 2020, Foulstone Road

Today I'm taking a more direct route from Mortimer Road up onto Derwent Edge than following the Duke's Road. I'm going up Foulstone Road, a footpath that leads from Strines Bridge almost directly to Back Tor and Lost Lad. The path is lined with heather, bushy bilberry shrubs and tough tussocks of moorland grass. A huge woolly caterpillar, about eight centimetres long, orangey with black bands and white markings, inches its way across the stony path in front of me. It's a handsome creature that I often encounter in such localities, the larva of the oak eggar moth, which does not, as its name would suggest, live on oak trees but on heather!

From all directions of the moor come plaintive whistling calls, a high-pitched peeping sound that comes first from one location in the long grass, then another, sounding uncannily as though a ventriloquist is throwing his voice. They are the calls of golden plovers, the so-called 'Guardians of the Moors', certainly the smartest, most elegant bird on the moor. One hops out of hiding onto a nearby rock and continues calling, such a weak and feeble song, forlorn and melancholy, for such a showy individual, but what brazen full courtship plumage he sports, black throat and belly bordered with mottled white and a rich golden back and head with black markings. I would have no hesitation in calling this the iconic bird of the moorlands were it not for the fact that there are at least half a dozen other contenders for the title; curlew, meadow pipit, skylark, short-eared owl, wheatear and, of course, the hen harriers. Despite being classed as waders, golden plovers live inland throughout the year, their bright plumage becoming duller in the winter when they spend time in fields lower down the valley. Their Latin name, Pluvialis apricaria, incidentally seems somewhat contradictory since the first part comes from pluvia, meaning rain, as it was believed that plovers flocked when rain was imminent, whilst the species name, apricaria, means to bask in the sun.

One particularly curious fact about the golden plover is that it played a small part in the creation of one of the books that you most probably have on your shelf right now. The story goes that on tenth November 1951, Sir Hugh

Beaver, the managing director of the Guinness Breweries, went on a shooting party in County Wexford, Ireland and, after missing a shot at a golden plover, became involved in an argument over which was the fastest game bird in Europe, the golden plover or the red grouse. He soon discovered, however, that there was no book with which to settle arguments about records and realised that a book supplying the answers to this sort of question might prove popular. He therefore set about commissioning just such a book, later published as the first *Guinness Book of World Records*. It became a bestseller within months and hasn't been off the bookstore shelves since. The golden plover turns out to be the faster, by the way, just in case you haven't got your copy handy.

Higher up, the heather moor stretches away in all directions, square miles of wild moorland peatland at its midsummer driest and it's a very different environment from when I was last up here in winter when everywhere was sodden. The bright green young heather is already showing the purple buds that will burst into a haze across the moor in August and I'm reminded that heather's other name, ling, comes from the Norse word for fire. Maybe the Vikings were as familiar as we are becoming with moorland fires, 2019 being one of the worst on record with major fires ravaging huge areas of Marsden and Saddleworth Moors, only a few miles to the north of us. I find it sickening to think of the enormous and irreparable damage that can result to such a fragile and unique habitat from the careless and irresponsible lighting of fires on tinder dry moorland like this. It's difficult to conceive of anything more reckless than lighting one of those disposable barbeques in such a place, though that's most likely what caused the Marsden Moor fire. The person who did it may not even have been aware of the damage they had caused as there may not have initially been flames. Heat from the barbeque would be sufficient to cause the peat to begin to smoulder and the effect to travel underground before eventually beginning to blaze.

I soon reach the flag-stoned path that leads along the ridge of Derwent Edge. It's a northern extension of the more well-known Stanage Edge, one of the scarps that form an inward facing wall along the eastern side of the Peak District. Derwent Edge displays its own particular features, huge, rounded, almost dough-like sculptures called 'tors', like the similarly shaped features on Dartmoor. These, however, are not composed of Devon granite, they were formed from tough gritstone by the actions of wind, rain and frost over many centuries, though exactly how is still debated. The cotton mill flags lead several miles along the summit, past the gallery of sculptures that have acquired names based on a fancied resemblance; The Coach and Horses, The Wheel Stones, The Cakes of Bread and the Salt Cellar, but, as with all modern art you have to use your imagination.

Bert Ward and the Fight for Access

I'm fortunate that today I can take for granted the right to wander at will over these wide expanses that have been designated 'Open Access Land' under the 'The Countryside and Rights of Way Act 2000' but this right is relatively recent and we should not forget the many people who had to fight to achieve it. As the nineteenth century progressed fewer and fewer people had become able to access the traditionally open country of the moorlands. Although, under the 1826 'Bradfield Enclosure Act', passage along the ancient right of way across the moor that became known as 'The Duke's Road' had been safeguarded, it had been illegally closed to the public by the owner, the Duke of Norfolk, and patrolled by his gamekeepers. GHB Ward, founder of the Sheffield Clarion Ramblers, and indefatigable campaigner for the right of access to the moors, carried out research into this and rediscovered its legal status as an ancient right of way. During 1931, in a bid to reassert this access across the moor, Ward with fellow members set about building the series of stone cairns that still stand along the ancient path.

The following year the Sheffield Ramblers' Federation took up the challenge of asserting what they saw as their right to roam freely and set about organising a mass trespass along the route. And so, on Sunday 18th September 1932 several hundred walkers assembled at Malin Bridge before heading up the Loxley Valley towards the Dukes Road, intent on walking on to Back Tor and return back to Malin Bridge. Several months previously a stir had been caused by the well-known 'Mass Trespass' on Kinder Scout and things were tense between walkers and land owners, so Ward himself decided not to take part as he did not wish to be associated with the same sort of violence as met the Kinder Scout trespassers. But all seemed to go well, with only the odd gamekeeper keeping an eye on them, until they reached the top of the moor overlooking Abbey Clough. Here about a hundred permanent and temporary gamekeepers, armed with pick-shafts, were gathered with a detachment of policemen, appointed to keep the peace. Although the Duke's men attempted to stop their progress and a small fracas ensued, the walkers held their ground and were allowed to proceed unhindered. Having made their point they sat down to eat their sandwiches before turning back whilst the gamekeepers vented their fury on the police for not making any arrests. This protest, one of many during the years of protest in favour of the 'Right to Roam', did not make the news nor the impact they probably desired, being overshadowed by the outcry that had followed the Kinder Mass Trespass and the imprisonment of the so-called ring leaders. Nonetheless, a further blow had been made on behalf of those who love to walk these moorlands.

The dogged agitators of groups like the Clarion Ramblers led by Ward and the Rambler's Association were mirrored in many of their aims by a very different group of Sheffield campaigners for the preservation of the countryside and the right to enjoy its benefits. In 1924, disturbed by what they saw as the 'defacement of the Peak District by incongruous development', a group of likeminded individuals, industrialists, academics, professionals and clergy met at Endcliffe Vale House in Sheffield with the idea of creating a society for its protection. The driving force behind the extraordinary achievements of the group was the husband-and-wife team of Ethel and Lt. Col. Gerald Haythornthwaite who steered the group from 1936 for the next fifty years. By 1927 the group had become affiliated to the CPRE, the Council for the Preservation of Rural England, and, as Chris Bonnington writes in the foreword to Mel Jones' book on the group's achievements:

> The group will go down in history as a major force in environmental conservation because of the achievement of its two 'grand purposes': the designation of a National Park in the Peak District and the creation of a permanent Sheffield Green Belt.

It's no coincidence that the Peak District was the first National Park to be designated in 1951. Both these remarkable achievements continue to have a profound influence on the valley and its way of life.

The fight for full access to the moorlands was, however, far from won. It was not until 1956 that the West Riding County Council made the decision to restore the Duke's Road as a public right of way under the 1949 National Parks and Access to the Countryside Act and so I thank them for granting to me and everyone else the unhindered right to enjoy this remarkable walk. It's a right that was celebrated by SCAM, the 'Sheffield Campaign for Access to Moorland', a group that had been created in 1982 as part of the celebrations to commemorate fifty years since the Kinder Mass Trespass, when they recreated the trespass along Duke's Road. The group, under Terry Howard and my friend and fellow sword dancer Les Seaman amongst others, continued to campaign and organise trespasses across great areas of local moorlands that were still out of bounds; Big Moor, Bamford Moor and Strines Moor amongst others. For many of the members, including Sheffield City Councillors and local MPs, this was an ideological and political struggle which bore fruit when Parliament passed 'The Countryside and Rights of Way Act' in November 2000. Known as 'The Right to Roam' the Act provides for a new right of access on foot to areas of open areas of mountain (land over 600 metres) and moorland. Bert Ward's dream had finally been accomplished, though he didn't live to see it.

Moorland Tragedy, December 14th 1937

Most of the people that I greet as we pass along these moorland tracks are well prepared for the harsh conditions, kitted out in wind and waterproof clothing made from modern technical materials. But this was not always the case and the tragic and appalling fate of seventeen-year-old Nora Leary tells a story of the hazards that can face those who venture across these bleak moorlands ill-prepared. On December 14th 1937 Nora had set out with three companion members of Sheffield Associate Rambling Club, Margaret Dearnaley, aged nineteen, Albert Garfitt, aged twenty-five, and Fred Glaser, aged twenty-three, to walk over the moor from Ewden by way of Back Tor, planning to reach Derwent village, where they had ordered tea, at five. Nora, the youngest of the group, had only joined the club a couple of months previously but Fred Garfitt was an experienced rambler. It would be a strenuous walk but quite doable in reasonable conditions. In winter, however, when such an undertaking could be hazardous, it was potentially a different proposition.

Sure enough before they reached the summit of Back Tor the weather had worsened. A fierce wind had blown up across the moor and swept snow from the north. The young people, dressed in the usual manner of hikers at the time, in shirt, tie, jackets and overcoats, began to struggle in the cold and wet of the ever-deepening snow. The landscape became a featureless void and it was soon clear they were completely lost. Nora quickly tired and began to succumb to the freezing cold and wet, complaining that she needed a rest, sagging at the knees and falling on her face. She collapsed six or seven times as they struggled on for hours and eventually the boys had to virtually drag her whilst also supporting Margaret. The light began to fail and desperately they searched for somewhere to shelter for the night. Stumbling into a deep ditch they found it impossible to support the girls any further. Here there was some slight relief from the unremitting wind and they decided to wait it out until dawn. The snow, however, continued unabated, becoming a blizzard, filling their meagre shelter. Nora cried out for her mother and became delirious. She got up but they made her lie down again, moaning and groaning. *"Then suddenly she became quiet and I thought she was asleep. She had her arms around me,"* said Margaret Dearnaley, in her evidence to the inquest. Nora had lost consciousness and at some point in the night, she died.

When daylight came it was still snowing hard but the three of them decided to go for help, the two boys virtually carrying Margaret who was having difficulty walking. For an incredible ten gruelling hours they battled on through thick snow and swollen streams before reaching a farm where they left Margaret before struggling on to reach Broomhead Hall and raise the alarm.

As quickly as possible a search party was organised, which included gamekeepers, police and a reporter from the *Daily Independent*, and the two boys, after a brief rest, set off again as guides to find the ill-fated Nora. It was to be a strenuous trek for the nine-man party, at times wading waist deep through icy streams and bogs. Conditions were so poor that after two and a half miles it was impossible to proceed with the horse sleigh that they had brought in the hope of using it as a hearse on the return, and they abandoned it at a shepherd's hut. They plodded onwards for another four and a half miles, man-hauling the sled, at times buried shoulder deep in drifts, before finding the place where the body lay, close to the summit of Margery Hill. It took twenty minutes for the body, which had been frozen and covered with snow, to be dug out. The party trudged single file by lamplight, the two boys nearly collapsing with fatigue after their heroic forty-hour ordeal. One of the search party, Police-Sergeant Paradise, said that they were all exhausted when they reached the shepherd's hut. *"We had come to the end of our physical endurance,"* he said.

A photograph of the sad procession appeared in the paper the next day. It shows the rescue party going down Mortimer Road towards Broomhead Hall. A verdict of 'Death by Misadventure' was returned by the jury at the inquest later in Sheffield. They expressed their view that no blame should be attached to any of the rambling party whose companion died as they lay huddled up in a blizzard on the wild moors above the Loxley Valley.

Unfortunately this appalling event does not exhaust the contents of this particular drawer of our cabinet. There is yet another, more recent tragedy to relate which occurred during the vicious winter of 1947. It was late in that winter, on Friday February 21st, when William Walker of Walker Edge Farm, that stands in an isolated spot way over the hilltop above High Bradfield, set out from the family to make the journey over the hill and down to the Post Office in Low Bradfield to collect his pension and tobacco as was his usual habit. It was a journey of about three miles, mainly downhill. Having accomplished his mission, he set off to return in the steadily worsening weather. Before long a full blizzard had blown up and the snow deepened. When William did not arrive home as expected the family mustered friends and neighbours to conduct a search along his expected route home. As darkness fell they found no sign of him but persevered through the hours of darkness by the light of tilly lamps. He had, it turned out, decided to abandon his usual path and walk home along Walker Edge Road rather than brave the steep climb up the hill, and it was not until Sunday that his lifeless, frozen body was and brought home by horse sled.

September 14th 2020, along Mortimer Road

When Mortimer Road was built back in the eighteenth century the moorland was still open and unenclosed and there were none of the coniferous plantations that we pass through as we follow the road south. Even today it's a tortuous drive as the road plunges steeply up and down the wooded ravines of Emlin and Agden dykes and it's difficult to imagine making this journey across such open, bleak countryside by some sort of horse-drawn vehicle, especially in winter!

After a couple of miles a large house comes into view standing just above the road on the right, commanding a magnificent prospect right down the length of the valley. It's an imposing building of grand Victorian design, with two matching gabled wings and a square three storey tower at one end. On closer inspection it turns out to be in ruins. Only the outer shell remains intact. The roof is collapsing, the floors and the windows have already gone, but it is curiously marked on the O.S. map as 'Children's Home.'

By the middle of the nineteenth century the fresh air and the sporting attractions of the grouse moors had begun to attract members of a new class to the upper valley, newly-wealthy industrialists, especially from the Sheffield steel and cutlery trades. In May 1852 the sale of land on Mortimer Road, including 102 acres of ancient woodland and seven acres of grassland adjoining Bradfield Moor, was advertised in the *Sheffield Independent* newspaper by Mr Joseph Hammerton of nearby Walker House. It was suggested that this freehold estate would be the ideal place to build a summer residence and perfect to use as a 'shooting box' in winter. The offer was taken up by William Jessop, proprietor of the William Jessop Steel Works, as the estate at Thornsett Moor was ideally situated on the way to Manchester, where the company had opened a branch on Dale Street. There he built the grand, now ruinous house called 'Thornsett Lodge' (later the name was changed to Thornseat), in about 1855 as a summer retreat and, as he was a keen sportsman, for Sidney to use during the grouse shooting season.

We can imagine the grand Victorian house parties that were entertained at Thornsett during these years. In 1858, for instance, Jessop was entertaining a party of about fifty gentlemen for the 'Glorious Twelfth'. As he recorded in his diary the day didn't go exactly as they had hoped:

> The weather was beautifully fine, the sun being exceedingly powerful until towards two o'clock, when the clouds wore a threatening aspect, and the sound of distant thunder attracted the attention of those who were unprepared for a storm. Vivid flashes of lightning, followed by loud peals of thunder, shortly afterwards came in quick succession. About four o'clock the storm became so violent that the sportsmen were obliged to leave the moors. The rain and hail stones descended heavily for a couple of hours and then somewhat abated, the storm apparently travelling in the direction of Sheffield.

When Sidney died in January 1871, his brother Thomas Jessop, who lived at Endcliffe Grange in Sheffield, was left the sole proprietor of William Jessop and Sons and now inherited the estate. He went on to become Master Cutler of the Company of Cutlers as well as serving as Mayor of Sheffield at the time of the 1864 flood and used part of his wealth to found and build the maternity hospital that still bears his name. He died in 1887 and Thornsett was inherited by his son, William Jessop, a keen sportsman and member of the Bradfield Game Association. He dearly loved the lodge and made it his permanent home. It was said that whenever he came to stay there he would order his chauffeur to let the tyres of his early car down so that he could use a foot-pump to refill them with good, moorland air! It was here that he spent the last twelve months of his life, and here he died on 4 July 1905.

His son, Thomas had little interest in the lodge and in 1908 the house was advertised to let on a yearly tenancy. It was described as having three reception rooms, twelve bedrooms, excellent servants' offices, extensive stabling and outbuildings. It also came with relatively rare electric light installation and all modern conveniences. In 1928 Sheffield auctioneers were instructed to sell all the contents of the house and in 1934 the hall was sold to Sheffield Corporation to be used as offices for the waterworks department who were responsible for the nearby reservoirs.

At the onset of the war in May 1939 it was announced that Thornsett Lodge would house infants from Herries Road Nursery 'in case of emergency' and this was exactly what happened, the children enjoying the fresh country air while the city below suffered at the hands of German bombers. This was the start of a long association between the lodge and children because when peace returned the building was used as an adjunct to Sheffield Corporation's 'Cottage Homes' orphanage at Fulwood. It was also around this time that the name appears to have been changed to Thornseat Lodge. A swimming pool was built at the rear of the house and in 1973 it had become a mixed-sex home for sixteen emotionally disturbed or 'difficult' children of all ages. The 1980s, however, were difficult for Sheffield. Unemployment was high, and the council was cash-strapped. There was little else to do but mothball it until better times came along. In the early 1990s it was used for a short time by the Sheffield Gingerbread Group as a place for families on low incomes to go and stay, but, with no money for upkeep, the house quickly fell into a state of disrepair.

The worse it became the less likely anybody was going to be interested in buying the property. In 1994 there were plans to turn the lodge into a possible location for an eight-place secure unit but hesitancy by Sheffield City Council and opposition from the Peak National Park meant plans were shelved and in 2004 the council finally sold the property to Hague Plant Excavations Ltd. whose ownership and intentions for this site and others that they own in the valley have been subject of much controversy ever since. Nothing was done to stop the rot and Thornseat Lodge now stands as a perilous ruin. Without listed status, its future is uncertain but it is now well beyond any hope of restoration. The ruins have attracted some curious interest. Recent internet posts of videos have been made by so called 'paranormal investigators' on the site at night with dubious pieces of equipment, calling the names of children in an effort to 'contact' some of the previous occupants of the house.

In an extraordinary recent twist to this sad tale, in June 2016 a new company was formed called Thornseat Lodge Ltd. who now offer the opportunity to hire a location adjoining the ruins of the lodge as a luxury wedding venue. Their advertising states:

You choose; tipi, yurt or marquee. Set in our stunning location overlooking the Peak District, Strines and Dale Dyke reservoirs and surrounding moorland. Parking for 100 cars. Luxury loos. Immense views. Fully stocked bar. Highly trained floor team. Excellent customer service. Thornseat Weddings offers all of this at our exclusive use wedding venue on the outskirts of Sheffield within the Peak District.

It's quite difficult to reconcile the advertising with the sad ruin that stands decaying here beside the Mortimer Road.

Mortimer Road continues through the coniferous plantations of the Wentworth Estate before diving down one side of the oak-wooded Strines Dyke and steeply up the other. As we come to the top of the hill a curious stone stands at the edge of the road. It is locally known as the 'Take-Off Stone', and indeed, these are the words carefully inscribed on it. It harks back to the early days of the road when, in order to negotiate steep inclines, an attendant with extra horses could be hired at the bottom of the hill that could be hitched to a wagon. The inscribed stone marked the exact spot at which the extra horses were to be unhitched, therefore avoiding any disputes about under or overcharging.

Today I pull in at the pub carpark on the opposite side of the road. It must have been a welcome sight to weary travellers who put up here for the night having withstood a freezing winter journey by coach over the moors and it's an equally welcome sight on this glorious late summer day. The Strines Inn, the only public house left in the upper dale, stands in a commanding position overlooking the head of the valley, at a height of 1000 feet above sea level, hard up against the moor, the most remote pub in Sheffield. A grove of venerable ancient sycamore trees shades the car park, their scaly, dragon-skin bark stained bright green and yellow with lichen and mosses. We sit down at one of the wooden picnic tables and order a ploughman's and a pint of Guinness and take in the view straight down the valley, the Strines and Dale Dyke reservoirs reflecting the dark, rich blue of today's sky. It's an extremely attractive building and a great pub, one of its attractions being the colourful, if rowdy, collection of peacocks that are particularly partial to a dropped chip or bit of a sandwich. The pub's website claims that *"The building that now houses Strines Inn was originally a manor house built in 1275"* but there is little to substantiate this date and it was certainly never a 'manor house'. Looking at the building it's clear that there have been any number of building phases. It's probable that the central core of the original gritstone farm building with its stone slated roof, dates from the seventeenth century, although there was most probably an earlier building on the site, with an upper wing added in the eighteenth century, and the part next to the road constructed in 1860. It was one of the properties of the Worralls, the local family from Ughill whose aspirations to the gentry is clearly demonstrated for all to see by their coat of arms carved above the doorway of the gabled porch. It's been overpainted with white paint so many times that the complex design of rampant lion with three goblets, and a winged hand holding a cross, is now indistinct.

In 1771 the farmhouse was converted to a public house by Anthony Worrall to accommodate all the expected travellers along the new turnpike, and long may it continue to do so. Our morris and sword dance team used to enjoy performing for the visitors here on summer evenings but as it got late, and the sun began to sink below the moor above, the midges would emerge in swarms and force us to perform only hanky dances and the poor musicians would be bitten to death before we all retreated inside for a sing!

August 1st 2020, The Duke's Road

I'm tramping back along the Duke's Road on a quest. Not since the Tour de France attracted thousands of visitors to the valley has there been such a buzz of excitement here. It's not only the twitchers that have been buzzing but the national press and media are all a twitch as well, and it's all because of a bird; but what a bird, a lammergeier or bearded vulture, only the second that has ever been spotted in this country. Not that it's difficult to spot, having a wingspan of some eight feet, a short, diamond-shaped tail and a feathery tuft under its chin, it's not like any bird you've ever seen. It appeared in this country in June, having been spotted in Belgium earlier in the year, before making its way north and settling down in late July on a rocky outcrop on Howden Edge, at the head of the Derwent Valley to our west, his shoulders hunched sulkily. Word soon got out and quickly he attracted huge numbers of birders with telescopic lenses and khaki anoraks with lots of pockets to follow the paths onto the moor from Derwent or Strines; so many that the police were forced to close the road for a while. Hundreds of cameras clicked as he spread his huge wings, took off, and circled on outspread wings, rising on a morning current, accompanied by a mobbing party of buzzards, which he dwarfed.

The photographs of the bird soaring lazily above the Loxley Valley on the internet are spectacular and I'm hoping to get to Back Tor from which vantage point it should be possible to look across towards Howden Edge and with any luck spot him on the move. It's a fine day but cool for midsummer, bright with scudding white clouds and a fierce wind that threatens to drive rain from the west. I have a promising start to the day as a red kite, by no means a regular visitor up here, sours high above as I drive to the head of the valley. Along the Duke's Road the moor is quiet, completely quiet, not a single bird call all morning, not even the usual 'go back, go back' from a grouse. Perhaps they have a long memory and, recognising the date, they are all hunkering down. After all, August 1st was, prior to 1772, the original date of the opening of the shooting season. When Parliament decided on the adoption of the Gregorian calendar eleven days were 'lost' and the 'Glorious Twelfth' became the opening day. Today there's only a few meadow pipits accompanying me on my four-mile walk. One lands on the path, flicking his tail ten metres in front of me as I walk along. As I get closer he takes off and lands another ten metres along the path. Several times he repeats this manoeuvre, accompanying me until deciding to fly off into the heather.

The interest in the vulture is not surprising as even in his homeland of the Alps or Pyrenees he would be a celebrity, there being fewer than a thousand in Europe where the bird's German name has done it immense disservice over the centuries. 'Lammergeyer' means 'lamb-eater', an entirely erroneous description of the bird since its diet is carrion and its feeding habits have given it an iconic, almost mythic reputation. It feeds almost exclusively on bones which it picks up in its talons, flies high, and drops onto a rock in the hope that they shatter so that it can reach the rich marrow. This behaviour has earned the bird the alternative name of 'bone breaker'.

Mary Queen of Scots, during her dreary and interminable fourteen years of captivity in Sheffield at the castle or Manor Lodge often consoled herself by spending hour after hour sewing embroideries with Bess of Hardwick and her maids. For many of these they chose subjects from books of natural history that were being produced at the time, their favourite being the literally wonderful, five volume *Historia Animalium* by Swiss author Conrad Gessner. As well as the beautiful illustrations of animals, birds and fish that he depicts, he includes drawings of fabulous animals that had been reported by travellers from far off lands. So, amongst the collection of Mary's embroidered panels surviving in the V&A and at Oxburgh Hall in Norfolk are the unicorn, various sea monsters and mermaids and two images of the lammergeyer, one copied directly from Gessner's image and labelled 'A Stork of the Montayns' and another labelled 'A Bon Brek'. The image is unmistakably the lammergeyer, depicted wings outstretched, with two white bones in his claws.

As far as wildlife Agencies like the RSPB are concerned the arrival of this remarkable bird in this location throws a more than welcome spotlight on something that has been a major concern for years; the local persecution of birds of prey. *"There are obvious concerns for the bird's safety"*, said Mark Thomas, the head of investigations at the RSPB, *"as it's currently within the worst ten kilometre square for raptor persecution in England, dominated by land used for driven grouse shooting."* He is referring to serious accusations that have been levelled against the employees of shooting estates by wildlife agencies, who point to their efforts of 'controlling vermin' in order to protect young nesting game birds. In particular they cite illegal practices of some gamekeepers as being responsible for the demise of certain birds of prey, such as the hen harrier and, in this area, the goshawk. In 2006 the RSPB was to comment cryptically in a special report called 'Peak Malpractice' that, *"The northern moorland area of the Peak District National Park is known as the Dark Peak. Sadly for birds of prey, it's very dark indeed."*

Take the goshawk. Goshawks were once widespread in British woodlands, but, in 1883, became the first raptor to be persecuted to extinction in Britain.

However, following unofficial releases by falconers, goshawks regained a foothold in the Peak District in the 1960s in the woodlands between Sheffield and Holmfirth and a small population slowly grew. The birds were elusive but during the 1970s and '80s keen birdwatchers were drawn to the area to catch a glimpse of them. Since then, however, there has been a dramatic change in their fortunes, and in 1999 it became apparent that several nests had failed for no obvious reason. From a well-established population of seven to eleven nesting pairs in the 1990s, it became evident that the species had been lost as a breeding bird from the woodlands around these moors by 2002. The local fortunes of peregrine falcons have suffered a similarly tragic course.

There is reason to hope, however, that the work of the Wildlife Trust and Yorkshire Water to maintain suitable habitat is bearing fruit, for 2019 saw the return of a breeding pair of goshawks to the Sheffield Lakelands. They laid four eggs and reared three young, of which two successfully fledged over the summer. Maybe, one day I will spot one of these emblematic birds. There is similar hope for the prospects of the hen harrier, 'The Skydancer', for in 2018 and 2019 they have successfully bred on National Trust moorland in the Dark Peak. This is very encouraging news indeed. It's early days, of course, but the fact the harriers have been 'allowed' to settle for a breeding attempt is a vast improvement in this part of the Peak District National Park, where two years ago it was reported that an armed gamekeeper, since prosecuted, was using a decoy hen harrier in what was widely believed to be an attempt to attract in, and then shoot, any prospecting hen harriers. *"Although there is only one bearded vulture here there are lots of other raptors"*, says Keith Tomkins, Sheffield Lakeland Landscape Partnership Programme Manager, *"I have been lucky enough to see merlin, hobbies, peregrines, harriers, buzzards and even goshawk while out and about, but unfortunately there are nowhere near as many as there should be. We need highlights such as this visit from the bearded vulture to raise more awareness of our birds of prey and the potential for our moorlands to be home to so many more of these magnificent birds."*

As Liz Ballard, Chief Executive of Sheffield and Rotherham Wildlife Trust says;

> We should all be able to see amazing birds of prey like Goshawk,
> Hen Harriers and Short Eared Owls when we walk across our
> Sheffield Moors. They are part of nature as well as our own heritage
> and culture.

I think we can all say a sincere 'amen' to that, but, whilst so-called 'sportsmen' are willing to pay well over £2000 a day for the privilege of killing a few grouse on our moors, there are powerful interests that will wish to preserve the status quo.

I'm getting to the level summit of the moor where the heather thins out and the white tufts of cotton grass wave in the stiff breeze. A tall cairn built of small gritstone boulders marks where the footpath down Abbey Brook, towards Howden, veers off. Two men stand in the heather a few yards away, binoculars pointing to the sky. *"Hello, are you looking for the vulture?"* I say, unnecessarily, not sure of my reception. They reply that they are, but don't seem very bothered. *"Have you spotted him today?"* I ask. *"No,"* they reply, *"He's not here. Someone got too near and disturbed him and he's flown off down the Hope Valley."*

Oh well, I'm so pleased to have seen the red kite today, and I retrace my path and drive down through Bradfield and back down the valley.

Selected References

Armitage, Ella 'A Key to English Antiquities' 1897.

Armitage, Harold 'Early Man in Hallamshire' 1939.

Battye, Ray 'The Forgotten Mines of Sheffield' ALD Design and Print,2004.

Bentley, David 'The Sheffield Hanged' ALD Design and Print, 2002.

Dyson, Michael, 'The Roman Diploma' 2017, Peak District National Park.

Bradfield Historical Society 'Bygones of Bradfield' Vols 1,2 and 3

Castle, Joe, 'A Look at Life in Bradfield Dale and the Surrounding Area from the High Middle Ages' 2008, Northend. 'Wadsley Top Feasts and Sermons' 'Candles, Corves and Clogs'

Crossley, David, 'Water Power on Sheffield's Rivers' University of Sheffield 1989.

Derry, John, 'The Story of Sheffield' 1910

Dungworth, Bradfield and District Heritage Group 'Remembering the Forgotten Heroes of the Parish of Bradfield' 2018

Dungworth, Storrs and District Local History Group, 'A Walk into History'

Harlow, Ian, 'The Holmfirth Floods' 2004, ALD Design and Print.

Hey, David, 'A History of the South Yorkshire Countryside', 2015

'A History of the Peak District Moors', 2014

'Historic Hallamshire', 2001

Hunter, Joseph, 'Hallamshire' 1819

Jones, Melvin, 'Protecting the Beautiful Frame', 2001.

Machan, Peter, 'The Dramatic Story of the Sheffield Flood', ALD Design and Print, 1999

Miller, W.T. 'The Watermills of Sheffield' 1928

Nunn, Malcolm, 'Around Bradfield, Loxley and Hillsborough' Tempus, 1996

Rolt, J.C. 'Robin Hood' 1982, Thames and Hudson.

Ryder, Peter, 'Timber Framed Buildings in South Yorkshire' South Yorkshire County Council, 1975

Sissons,David, 'Right To Roam' Northend, 2005.

Smith, Dennis, 'Crafts of old Bradfield in the seventeenth and eighteenth Centuries'

'The Cutlery Industry in the Stannington Area,' 1977

Smith, Howard, 'Mortimer Road, The Turnpike that Failed' 1993.

Stannington Local History Group, 'Stannington' 1974. 'Stannington, A Year' by Joseph Atkins 'The Stannington Hunt' 'Stannington in 1851' by N.E. Reaney

In addition many internet sites have been consulted. The following sites have been particularly helpful;-

Chris Hobb's site on Sheffields history; www.chrishobbs.com

Sheffield Lakeland Landscape Partnership site; www.wildsheffield.